Copyright Issues Relevant to Digital Preservation and Dissemination of Pre-1972 Commercial Sound Recordings by Libraries and Archives

Commissioned for and sponsored by the National
Recording Preservation Board, Library of Congress

by June M. Besek
December 2005

Council on Library and Information Resources
and Library of Congress
Washington, D.C.

The National Recording Preservation Board

The National Recording Preservation Board was established at the Library of Congress by the National Recording Preservation Act of 2000. Among the provisions of the law are a directive to the Board to study and report on the state of sound recording preservation in the United States. More information about the National Recording Preservation Board can be found at http://www.loc.gov/rr/record/nrpb/.

ISBN 1-932326-23-5
ISBN 978-1-932326-23-9
CLIR Publication No. 135

Copublished by:

Council on Library and Information Resources
1755 Massachusetts Avenue, NW, Suite 500
Washington, DC 20036
Web site at http://www.clir.org

and

Library of Congress
101 Independence Avenue, SE
Washington, DC 20540
Web site at http://www.loc.gov

Additional copies are available for $20 per copy. Orders must be placed through CLIR's Web site.
This publication is also available online at no charge at http://www.clir.org/pubs/abstract/pub135abst.html.

♾ The paper in this publication meets the minimum requirements of the American National Standard for Information Sciences—Permanence of Paper for Printed Library Materials ANSI Z39.48-1984.

Contents

About the Author

June M. Besek is executive director of the Kernochan Center for Law, Media and the Arts at Columbia Law School, where she conducts research on copyright law, particularly as it relates to new technologies. She also teaches seminars on Authors, Artists and Performers and on Advanced Topics in Copyright. She is the author of many articles on copyright law issues. Ms. Besek serves as a consultant to the Library of Congress in connection with the National Digital Information Infrastructure and Preservation Program (NDIIPP) initiative, and as a member of the Section 108 Study Group, convened by the Library of Congress to reexamine existing library privileges under the Copyright Act and consider what amendments may be appropriate in light of the changes wrought by digital media. Ms. Besek holds a law degree from New York University School of Law and a B.A. in economics from Yale University.

Foreword

Enactment of the National Recording Preservation Act of 2000 came at an auspicious time for the Library of Congress and other sound recording archives and libraries. The U.S. Congress recognized that preservation responsibilities of institutions holding audio collections were increasing as collections grew, and that authoritative information was required by archives to assure the survival of their collections. When Congress created the National Recording Preservation Board in this law, it charged the Board with conducting a study of the state of audio preservation in the United States. The law also directed the Library of Congress to create a comprehensive national plan for audio preservation. The findings of this study will inform that preservation plan.

The preservation study, of which this publication is the second installment, is examining a range of issues identified by Congress in the Recording Preservation legislation: the emergence of standards for digital preservation; guidelines for reformatting at-risk recordings; U.S. copyright laws that affect audio preservation; and how scholars and the public might access historical recordings legally.

Congress specifically mandated that the study examine "copyright and other laws applicable to the preservation of sound recordings." Presently, the relation of federal copyright law to recorded sound is receiving a great deal of attention. Laws are scrutinized, challenged, and revised in response to the ease with which digital recordings can be duplicated. Yet, sound recordings produced in the United States prior to 1972—over 80 years of recorded sound history—are not protected by federal copyright law. Rather, they are protected by a combination of state copyright laws and federal laws that govern the musical or other works performed on the recordings.

June Besek's study lucidly summarizes how audio preservation is affected by state and other laws. A number of laws impact how we may preserve recordings and what we may do with the copies we create. This work examines these laws within the context of preservation and provides an analysis that will be useful to the legal community as well as to archivists.

The laws governing sound recordings made before 1972 are not simple and, as this study implies, some may in fact impede effective preservation. Without this work we would not be aware of the challenges implicit in the laws and understand their full impact. This report will be of great value in creating a national preservation plan. We are grateful to Congress for supporting this significant work and to June Besek for bringing light and clarity to a complex topic.

James H. Billington
Librarian of Congress

Preface

Since the beginning of commercial sound recording in the 1890s, Americans have been enthusiastic creators and prolific consumers of recordings. Almost every form of sound has been captured—from musical performances and whale songs to political addresses and oral histories. Entrepreneurs of the late nineteenth century created a consumer market for recordings, and the commercial sector has played a significant role in the growth of the recording industry and the innovation of recording technologies. Despite the popularity of sound, however, federal copyright was not extended to sound recordings until 1972. State laws protect all recordings produced before that date.

It is those state laws that libraries and archives must follow when making decisions about copying their fragile historical recordings in order to preserve them. Sophisticated tools for rerecording offer a means to copy fragile wax cylinders or lacquer discs once and forever. As a result, many libraries today can retire original copies from use and, at the same time, broaden access to these valued materials through the use of digital surrogates. But do these laws allow them to do that?

This report by June Besek addresses the question of what libraries and archives are legally empowered to do to preserve and make accessible for research their holdings of pre-1972 commercial recordings, the large aural legacy that is not protected by federal copyright. The report is one of a series of studies undertaken by the National Recording Preservation Board, under the auspices of the Library of Congress, to "maintain and preserve sound recordings that are culturally, historically, or aesthetically significant," as directed by Congress in the National Recording Preservation Act of 2000 [Public Law 106-474]. The act specifically requires the conduct of a study of "[c]urrent laws and restrictions regarding the use of archives of sound recordings, including recommendations for changes in such laws and restrictions to enable the Library of Congress and other nonprofit institutions in the field of sound recording preservation to make their collections available to researchers in a digital format" and of "[c]opyright and other laws applicable to the preservation of sound recordings." Ms. Besek's study, together with a forthcoming second study, which will focus on the rights associated with unpublished recordings, will provide essential information to the Library of Congress when it develops its national plan for preserving sound recordings, as the law provides.

As the first in-depth analysis by a nationally known expert in copyright law, this report will also be a timely and authoritative aid to the many librarians and archivists who face decisions daily about how to establish priorities for sound preservation. This report not only provides clear evidence of the need for updating copyright law to take advantage of digital technologies to preserve and to make accessible the full range of our sound heritage, but also demonstrates what preserving institutions can do to ensure access to our past aural landscape into the future.

Samuel Brylawski
Consultant to the National Recording Preservation Board
Library of Congress

Abby Smith
Consultant to the Council on Library and Information Resources

1. Introduction

The purpose of this study is to analyze copyright and related rights issues involved in the digital preservation and dissemination of pre-1972 commercial sound recordings by libraries and archives, focusing on the scope of protection for those recordings and on allowable uses, particularly for research and scholarship.

Copyright law as it relates to sound recordings and musical compositions is extremely complex. This complexity results both from historical and political factors and from the particular challenges presented by new technological means of disseminating music.

There are generally two separate works embodied in a sound recording. The first work is the sound recording itself, that is, the "fixation of a series of musical, spoken, or other sounds."[1] The second is referred to as the "underlying work," which, in the case of pre-1972 commercial sound recordings, is commonly a musical composition (a piece of music, with or without lyrics). It can, however, be a different kind of work, such as a humorous monologue or dialogue, a poem, a short story, a play, or a foreign-language lesson. Analyzing rights in a sound recording requires consideration not only of the rights in the sound recording itself but also of those in the underlying work. More than one sound recording may be based on a particular underlying work. For example, many artists have recorded Cole Porter's *Begin the Beguine*. There may be more than one underlying work for a particular sound recording. For example, there are different poems, published at different times, that underlie the Robert Frost recording in example 3, below.

---

[1] "Sound recordings" are defined in the Copyright Act as "works that result from the fixation of a series of musical, spoken, or other sounds, but not including the sounds accompanying a motion picture or other audiovisual work, regardless of the nature of the material objects, such as discs, tapes or other phonorecords, in which they are embodied." 17 U.S.C. § 101. Copyright law is contained in Title 17 of the United States Code (U.S.C.). All statutory references in this paper are to sections of Title 17, unless otherwise noted.

Copyright © 2005 June M. Besek, Kernochan Center for Law, Media and the Arts, Columbia Law School. Many thanks to Robert Clarida, Jane Ginsburg, Fred Koenigsberg and Eric Schwartz for their helpful comments and suggestions on drafts of this report. Research assistance from Zainab Ahmad, Tom Paskowitz, Rupa Rao, Mark Rasmussen and Maria Termini, all members of the Columbia Law School class of 2005, is gratefully acknowledged.

Prior to 1972, federal copyright law did not protect sound recordings.[2] The key date is February 15, 1972: sound recordings first fixed in a tangible medium of expression (e.g., recorded on disc or tape) on or after that date are protected by federal copyright law. Sound recordings first fixed before that date ("pre-1972 sound recordings") continue to be protected by a patchwork of state laws, civil and criminal, until 2067. There is, however, an exception to this rule: certain pre-1972 sound recordings of *foreign* origin are protected by federal copyright law, as will be explained below. Regardless of whether sound recordings were first fixed before or after February 15, 1972, the underlying musical or other works are governed by federal copyright law (unless they are in the public domain).

This report begins with a general discussion of federal copyright law and of state laws that govern sound recordings. That discussion is followed by a more specific legal analysis of preservation and dissemination activities with respect to sound recordings.

To illustrate some of the legal principles and practices discussed in this report, we will refer at various points to the following examples of sound recordings:[3]

> *Example 1*: *White Christmas*, recorded by Bing Crosby in 1942. The underlying musical composition, by Irving Berlin, was written in 1942.

> *Example 2*: Mahler's *Symphony No. 5*, recorded in 1947 by the New York Philharmonic, conducted by Bruno Walter.

> *Example 3*: Poems by Robert Frost, as read by Robert Frost, recorded in 1956. Frost died in 1963. The poems were copyrighted at various times, some prior to 1923, some later.

> *Example 4*: Telemann's *Suite in E-Minor*, recorded in 1952 in England by the Goldsbrough Orchestra, conducted by Arnold Goldsbrough.

---

[2] The kinds of works on which sound recordings are typically based have been protected by copyright far longer. Books were included in the first copyright act in 1790; musical compositions were added in 1831.

[3] All these sound recordings were first recorded in the United States, unless otherwise noted. These examples are provided merely for the sake of discussion and in some cases are based on assumptions: (1) We are assuming that *White Christmas* was distributed in sheet music (with copyright notice) in 1942, although we have not checked the copyright registration to determine the publication date. (2) *Symphony No. 5* was written in 1901–1902; we assume that it was published shortly thereafter. Mahler died in 1911. (3) We didn't try to sort out the copyright dates for all of the various poems read, which spanned many years. It is clear, however, that the poems read were copyrighted under the 1909 act and that some remain copyright protected. (4) The Goldsbrough Orchestra (which later became the English Chamber Orchestra) did record Telemann's *Suite in E-Minor* sometime in the period 1948–1952, but we don't know for certain that it was 1952. The precise year is irrelevant for purposes of this illustration. (5) This was one of the works at issue in the *Capitol Records v. Naxos* case, discussed in section 3.3 of this report. (6) Finally, we are assuming (but have not verified) that the musical compositions underlying examples 2 (Mahler), 4 (Telemann), and 5 (Bach) are in the public domain, and that the recordings did not involve new copyrighted arrangements of these compositions.

Example 5: J. S. Bach's *Cello Suites*, recorded between 1936 and 1939 in England by Pablo Casals.

Example 6: *Like a Virgin*, recorded by Madonna in 1984. The underlying musical composition was written by Billy Steinberg and Tom Kelly in 1984.

2. U.S. Copyright Law

Even though federal copyright law does not apply directly to most pre-1972 sound recordings, it is relevant to this report in several respects: (1) as indicated above, certain pre-1972 sound recordings of foreign origin are governed by federal copyright law; (2) many sound recordings embody musical or other underlying works that are protected by federal copyright law; and (3) our review of state law, discussed below, suggests that some states may evaluate state law claims relating to pre-1972 sound recordings with reference to federal copyright law.

2.1 Protected Works

"Copyright" exists in any original work of authorship that is fixed in a tangible medium, such as paper, canvas, or a computer disc. For a work to be "original," it must meet two qualifications: (1) it cannot be copied from another work; and (2) it must exhibit at least a small amount of creativity.

Copyright protects a wide range of works. The principal categories for works of authorship are as follows:
- literary works
- musical works, including any accompanying words
- dramatic works, including any accompanying music
- pantomimes and choreographic works
- pictorial, graphic, and sculptural works
- motion pictures and other audiovisual works
- sound recordings
- architectural works

Copyright does not protect all aspects of a work. Ideas, concepts, methods, principles, procedures, and the like may not be protected, although the specific manner in which they are expressed may be.

2.2 Term of Protection

The duration of copyright protection in the United States differs depending on when the work was created and published.

2.2.1 Term for All Works Created on or after January 1, 1978
For works first created on or after January 1, 1978 (the effective date of the current Copyright Act), copyright lasts for the life of the

author and 70 years thereafter.[4] For anonymous works and works made for hire,[5] the term is 95 years from publication or 120 years from creation, whichever expires first. So, for example, the musical composition *Like a Virgin* (example 6, above) will be protected for 70 years after the death of its last surviving author. The sound recording by Madonna—assuming it is a work made for hire, as sound recordings commonly purport to be—will be protected until 2079 (1984 plus 95 years).

2.2.2 Term for *Works Created* and *Published before January 1, 1978*

For works first published prior to January 1, 1978, the rules are more complicated, but can be summarized as follows.

Date first published with copyright notice[6]	Term of protection
Before 1923	Work is in the public domain.
1923–1963	If the copyright was renewed in the 28th year, the work is protected for a total of 95 years from publication. If the copyright was not renewed, the work is in the public domain.[7]
1964–1977	95 years from publication.

So, for example, if the copyright in Irving Berlin's composition *White Christmas* was renewed in 1970, as we assume it was (see example 1, above), the copyright in the song would expire at the end of 2037 (1942 plus 95 years).

2.2.3 Term for *Works Created* but not *Published before January 1, 1978*

If a work was created but not published before January 1, 1978, it has been given the same term as works created on or after January 1, 1978: life of the author plus 70 years, or, for anonymous works and works made for hire, 95 years from creation or 120 years from publication. However, all works unpublished as of January 1, 1978, no matter how old, were protected under the law at least until Decem-

---

[4] § 302(a).

[5] A "work made for hire" is a work created by an employee in the course of his or her employment, or a commissioned work where the commissioning party and the creator agree in writing that the product will be a work made for hire. Only certain categories of works are eligible to be commissioned works made for hire. § 101. If a work qualifies as a work made for hire, the employer or commissioning party is considered the author and owns all rights, unless the parties agree otherwise in a signed writing. § 201(b).

[6] A work is considered "published" when copies are distributed to the public "by sale or other transfer of ownership, or by rental, lease or lending. The offering to distribute copies . . . to a group of persons for purposes of further distribution, public performance, or public display, constitutes publication. A public performance or display of a work does not of itself constitute publication." § 101.

Under the 1909 Copyright Act, publication with notice was required to qualify for federal protection. A work published without notice went into the public domain. The notice requirement was eliminated by the Berne Convention Implementation Act of 1988.

[7] Certain works of foreign origin whose copyrights were not renewed may have had their copyrights restored. See discussion in section 2.6 of this report.

ber 31, 2002. If a work that was unpublished as of January 1, 1978, was published between that date and December 31, 2002, its term of protection will not end until December 31, 2047.[8]

Intuitively, it would seem that pre-1972 *commercial* sound recordings would be considered "published" both as to the sound recording and the underlying work, but this is not necessarily the case. Under copyright law, a performance of a work is not deemed a publication, so playing the work live or on the radio is not "publication." If, for example, as part of a "young artists" program, a radio station records and broadcasts a classical music concert by Julliard students, the station does not "publish" that recording, regardless of how many people listen to the broadcast. The students' renditions would not be deemed "published" until phonorecords (the technical name for copies of sound recordings) are distributed to the public "by sale or other transfer of ownership, or by rental, lease or lending."[9] Moreover, even musical compositions commercially distributed in phonorecords may not be "published" under the law. Because of a dispute over the copyright status of certain musical compositions distributed on phonorecords without copyright notice, Congress amended the Copyright Act in 1997 to provide that "[t]he distribution before January 1, 1978 of a phonorecord shall not for any purpose constitute a publication of the musical work embodied therein."[10] So, if the underlying musical work was distributed in another format, such as sheet music, it was published; if not, it was unpublished at January 1, 1978, and received the term of protection described above for unpublished works. The law is ambiguous about whether the distribution

---

[8] All works unpublished at January 1, 1978, were given at least 25 years of federal copyright protection (that is, until December 31, 2002), but those that were published by December 31, 2002, were given 50 years of federal protection (until December 31, 2027). That date was extended by 20 years in the Sonny Bono Copyright Term Extension Act of 1998, so that those works published by the end of 2002 will remain protected under federal copyright law for a total of 70 years (until December 31, 2047).

[9] § 101.

[10] § 303(b). The law was passed because a significant number of phonorecords released before the current law took effect failed to include a copyright notice with respect to the underlying musical works, as many believed it was unnecessary as a matter of law and industry practice. Subsequently, some courts ruled that the distribution of phonorecords without notice under the 1909 Copyright Act injected the underlying musical works into the public domain. The 1997 amendment effectively extended the term of protection for some of the underlying musical works beyond what they would have had if they were published with notice on the phonorecord in the first instance. Melville D. Nimmer and David Nimmer, *Nimmer on Copyright*, § 4.05[B][2] at 429–32 (LexisNexis/Matthew Bender, 2004).

What constitutes a publication of a pre-1972 sound recording is a matter of state law, and states are "free to depart from the Copyright Act's definition of publication." Paul Goldstein, *Copyright*, § 15.5.2 at 15:45 (Aspen, 2nd ed., 2004). Publication status of pre-1972 sound recordings may not be critical to state law protection. For example, the California civil code (see section 3.4 of this report) provides protection on the basis of the date of fixation, not of publication. See *Capitol Records, Inc. v. Naxos of America, Inc.*, 4 N.Y.3d 540, 560 (2005). (In the absence of federal statutory protection, distribution of a sound recording "does not constitute a publication sufficient to divest the owner of common-law copyright protection.") (citations omitted).

of a phonorecord is a publication of the underlying work if that work is anything other than a musical composition (e.g., a spoken-word recording).[11]

2.3 Rights under Copyright

Copyright provides a copyright owner with a bundle of rights that can be exploited or licensed separately or together. In the case of a sound recording embodying a musical composition, each copyright owner has a separate bundle of rights. Those rights include the following:

1. *The reproduction right (i.e., the right to make copies).* A "copy" of a work can be any form in which the work is fixed, or embodied, and from which it can be perceived, reproduced, or communicated, either directly or with the aid of a machine.[12] Courts have held that even the reproduction created in the short-term memory (RAM) of a computer when a program is loaded for use qualifies as a copy.[13]

2. *The right to create adaptations (also known as "derivative works").* A "derivative work" is a work that is based on a copyrighted work but that contains new material that is "original" in the copyright sense. For example, the movie *To Kill a Mockingbird* is a derivative work of the book of the same name by Harper Lee. A new arrangement of a musical composition, or a new version of a song with updated lyrics, can be a derivative work if it contains sufficient original authorship.

3. *The right to distribute copies of the work to the public.* Making copies of a work available for public downloading over an electronic network qualifies as a public distribution.[14] The distribution right is limited by the "first sale doctrine," discussed below in section 2.4, "Privileges and Exceptions." Distribution may also be limited by a license (particularly with respect to copies of works distributed in digital form).

4. *The right to perform the work publicly.* To "perform" a work means to recite, render, play, dance, or act it, with or without the aid of

---

[11] The provision quoted in text does not, by its terms, apply to anything other than musical works. The courts were divided on this issue prior to the amendment, so the status of material underlying a spoken-word, pre-1972 sound recording distributed without copyright notice is unclear. Compare *La Cienega Music Co. v. ZZ Top*, 53 F.3d 950 (9th Cir.), *cert. denied*, 116 S. Ct. 331 (1995), with *Rosette v. Rainbo Record Mfg. Corp.*, 354 F. Supp. 1183 (S.D.N.Y. 1973), *aff'd*, 546 F.2d 461 (2d Cir. 1976).

[12] § 101.

[13] For example, *MAI Systems Corp. v. Peak Computer*, 991 F.2d 511 (9th Cir. 1993), *cert. dismissed*, 114 S. Ct. 671 (1994). In a 2001 report to Congress, the Copyright Office observed, "Every court that has addressed the issue of reproductions in volatile RAM has expressly or impliedly found such reproductions to be copies within the scope of the reproduction right." U.S. Copyright Office, *DMCA Section 104 Report* 118 (August 2001).

[14] See, for example, *New York Times Co. v. Tasini*, 533 U.S. 483, 498 (2001), stating that Lexis/Nexis, by selling copies of allegedly infringing materials through its database, is distributing copies to the public; Robert A. Gorman & Jane C. Ginsburg, *Copyright: Cases and Materials* 545–46 (Foundation Press, 6th ed., 2002).

a machine.[15] The meaning of the word "publicly" is discussed below. Thus, a live concert is a performance of a musical composition, and so, too, is playing a CD on which that composition is recorded. This general public-performance right does not extend to sound recordings, which have their own, narrowly tailored right of public performance (see paragraph 6, below).

5. *The right to display the work publicly.* To "display" a work means to show a copy of it, either directly or with the aid of a device or process.

6. *Performance right in sound recordings.* Copyright owners of sound recordings (principally recording artists and recording companies) do not enjoy the general right of public performance that attaches to most other works. Instead, they have a more limited right, which is "to perform the work publicly by means of a digital audio transmission." The contours of this right are described in section 2.6 of this report.

The word "publicly" as used to define certain copyright rights is a broad concept. To perform or display a work publicly means to perform or display it anywhere that is open to the public or anywhere that a "substantial number of persons outside of a normal circle of a family and its social acquaintances is gathered."[16] Transmitting the performance or display to such a place also makes it public. It does not matter whether members of the public receive the performance at the same time or at different times, at the same place or different places. Making a work available to be received or viewed by the public over an electronic network is a public performance or display of the work.[17] Broadcasting it over the radio is a public performance. Playing a CD in one's home for family and friends is a private performance.

Ownership of a copy of a work (even of the original copy, if there is only one) and ownership of the copyright rights are separate and distinct. For example, libraries and archives occasionally receive donations of vinyl discs or eight-track tapes, but they generally own only the physical copies and not the copyright rights.[18]

As the discussion of the performance right in sound recordings suggests, not all rights attach to all works. For example, some works, such as sculpture, are not capable of being performed. Other works—notably, musical compositions and sound recordings, discussed below—are subject to "compulsory licenses" for certain uses. A compulsory license is a specific legal authorization to use a copyrighted work (in other words, the copyright owner cannot deny per-

---

[15] § 101.

[16] *Id.*

[17] See, for example, *Playboy Enters., Inc. v. Frena*, 839 F. Supp. 1552 (M.D. Fla. 1993).

[18] A donor of physical material frequently does not own the rights and therefore cannot convey them. For example, the writer, not the recipient, owns the copyright in letters, though the recipient owns the physical copies. Even when the donor owns the rights, they are transferred to the library or archives only if the gift includes a license or an assignment. § 202.

mission to use it) in certain ways or for certain purposes, provided that the user pays the required fee and otherwise meets the conditions in the law.

2.4 Privileges and Exceptions

The Copyright Act contains many privileges and exceptions to the rights outlined above. Below is a brief description of the privileges and exceptions most relevant to digital preservation and dissemination by libraries and archives, followed by a discussion of aspects of the law specific to musical works and sound recordings. As discussed above, federal copyright law does not apply to most pre-1972 sound recordings. It does, however, govern certain pre-1972 sound recordings of foreign origin and many of the works that underlie pre-1972 sound recordings, even though the sound recordings themselves may not be protected by copyright. Federal copyright law is also indirectly relevant to pre-1972 U.S. recordings, to the extent that state court decisions concerning such recordings are informed by the scope of federal copyright protection.

2.4.1 Fair Use: § 107

Fair use is the best-known exception to copyright. Fair use excuses a use that would otherwise be infringing. There is no simple test for determining whether a use is fair. The law sets out four factors that must be evaluated in each case to determine whether a use is fair, although other factors may be considered.

1. *The purpose and character of the use.* Among the considerations is whether the use is commercial or for nonprofit, educational purposes. Works that transform or recast the original by adding new creative authorship are more likely to be considered fair use.[19] However, a use can be fair even if it is merely a reproduction, and a use that is transformative will not necessarily be considered fair.

2. *The nature of the copyrighted work.* The scope of fair use is generally broader for fact-based works than it is for fanciful or creative works, and broader for published works than for unpublished ones.

3. *The amount and substantiality of the portion of the work used in relation to the work as a whole.* Generally, the more that is taken, the less likely it is to be fair use, but there are situations in which making complete copies is considered fair.[20]

---

19 In some cases, courts have found that using a work for a different purpose provides a transformative element. See, for example, *Kelly v. Arriba Soft Corp.*, 336 F.3d 811, 819 (9th Cir. 2003) (low-resolution "thumbnail" photos in defendant's search engine database deemed transformative since they serve a different function—improving access to information on the Internet—than do the photos themselves, which were created for an artistic/aesthetic purpose).

20 For example, in *Sony Corp. of America v. Universal City Studios, Inc.*, 464 U.S. 417 (1984)—commonly referred to as the "Betamax case"—the Supreme Court held that private, in-home copying of free television programs for time-shifting purposes was fair use.

4. *The effect on the market for, or value of, the copyrighted work.* A use that usurps the actual or potential market for the original is unlikely to qualify as fair use.

Certain uses are favored in the statute: criticism, comment, news reporting, teaching (including multiple copies for classroom use), scholarship, and research. Preservation and dissemination by a non-profit digital library or archives for scholarly or research purposes would be the kind of use favored by the law. However, favored uses are not automatically deemed fair, and other uses are not automatically deemed unfair. There is no formula to determine whether a use is fair. The determination depends on the facts of a particular case. The factors discussed above must be considered in each case by the user and, if there is a dispute, by the courts.

2.4.2 Special Library Privileges: § 108

The Copyright Act contains a number of privileges specific to libraries and archives. To qualify for these privileges, the library or archives must be open to the public, or at least to researchers in a specialized field; the reproduction and distribution may not be for commercial advantage; and the library or archives must include a copyright notice on any copies provided.[21]

(a) Copying for Maintenance and Preservation

Section 108(b) allows libraries or archives to make up to three copies of an unpublished copyrighted work "solely for purposes of preservation and security or for deposit for research use in another library or archives." The work must be currently in the collections of the library or archives, and any copy made in digital format may not be made available to the public in that format outside the library premises.

Section 108(c) allows libraries and archives to make up to three copies of a published work to replace a work in their collections that is damaged, deteriorating, lost, or stolen, or whose format has become obsolete, if the library determines after reasonable effort that an unused replacement cannot be obtained at a fair price (the extent to which one library may rely on another to make copies is addressed in section 4.1.3 of this report). As with copies of unpublished works, copies in digital format may not be made available to the public outside the library premises.[22]

---

[21] Concerning the commercial aspect of archives, the legislative history of § 108 states:

> [A] purely commercial enterprise could not establish a collection of copyrighted works, call itself a library or archive, and engage in for-profit reproduction and distribution of photocopies. Similarly, it would not be possible for a non-profit institution, by means of contractual arrangements with a commercial copying enterprise, to authorize the enterprise to carry out copying and distribution functions that would be exempt if conducted by the non-profit institution itself.

H.R. Rep. No. 94-1476, 94th Cong., 2d Sess. 74 (1976) [hereinafter, *House Report*].

[22] § 108(c). In limiting use of digital copies made pursuant to this section to library premises, Congress appears to have ignored the possibility that the work may have been distributed to the public in digital form. In that case, the limitation to use on the premises introduces a restriction on use of the copies that may not have existed with the original.

Until the Digital Millennium Copyright Act (DMCA) was passed in 1998, the copying privileges in § 108(b) and (c) discussed above were limited to a single copy of a work "in facsimile form." The DMCA changed these provisions to permit up to three copies and to allow those copies to be made in digital form, in recognition of the changing practices of libraries and archives (particularly with respect to the use of digital technology). Many in the library community, however, would argue that Congress did not go far enough in expanding libraries' privileges to take advantage of digital technology.

(b) Copying for Library Patrons

Section 108 also allows libraries and archives, under certain conditions, to reproduce and distribute to patrons all or part of a copyrighted work. However, certain works—including musical works; pictorial, graphic, and sculptural works (other than illustrations or similar adjuncts to literary works); and audiovisual works (including motion pictures)—are not subject to these reproduction and distribution privileges.[23]

Specifically, a library or an archives may reproduce and distribute, in response to a user's request, "no more than one article or other contribution to a copyrighted collection or periodical issue," or "a small part" of any other copyrighted work from its collection or that of another library or archives. It may also copy all or a substantial portion of a user-requested work if it determines, after reasonable investigation, that a copy cannot be obtained at a fair price. However, these reproduction and distribution privileges have conditions: they apply only if "the library or archives has had no notice that the copy would be used for purposes other than private study, scholarship, or research"; the copy becomes the property of the requesting user (so the exemption does not become a means of collection building); and the library or archives displays a warning of copyright where it accepts orders.[24]

These exemptions encompass "isolated and unrelated reproduction or distribution of a single copy . . . of the same material on separate occasions."[25] They do not apply when a library or an archives "is aware or has substantial reason to believe that it is engaging in the related or concerted reproduction or distribution of multiple copies" of the same material, whether at one time or over a period of time. Likewise, they do not apply to a library or an archives that "engages in the systematic reproduction or distribution of a single or multiple copies" of a work. Libraries and archives may participate

---

[23] § 108(i). Audiovisual news programs are a separate category. See § 108(f)(3).

[24] §§ 108(d), (e). Section 108 does not impose any liability for copyright infringement on a library or an archives for the unsupervised use of reproduction equipment on its premises as long as the equipment displays a notice that "the making of a copy may be subject to the copyright law." § 108(f)(1). However, § 108 does not excuse someone who uses the reproduction equipment or requests a copy under § 108(d) "from liability for copyright infringement for any such act, or for any later use of such copy . . . , if it exceeds fair use as provided by section 107." § 108(f)(2).

[25] § 108(g).

in interlibrary arrangements as long as the practice is not intended to—and does not—substitute for a subscription to or purchase of the work.[26]

(c) Special-Use Provisions for the Last 20 Years of the Copyright Term

The copyright law contains a special provision for use of "orphan works" whose copyright owners cannot be located. The provision was passed as part of the 1998 Copyright Term Extension Act, which extended the copyright term by 20 years (from life of the author plus 50 years to life plus 70 years). A library or an archives may reproduce, distribute, perform, or display in facsimile or digital form a copy of a published work during the last 20 years of its term, for purposes of preservation, scholarship, or research. This privilege applies only if the work is not subject to normal exploitation and cannot be obtained at a reasonable price. To take advantage of this privilege, a qualified institution must first make a reasonable investigation to determine that the work meets these criteria and that the copyright owner has not filed a notice to the contrary in the Copyright Office.[27]

Until recently, the terms of the statute excluded musical works; most pictorial, graphic, and sculptural works; and audiovisual works (including motion pictures) from these special-use provisions. This exclusion was eliminated early in 2005 when Congress amended the Copyright Act to make all categories of works eligible in the last 20 years of their copyright term for broader use by libraries and archives.[28]

Even if copying a work is not expressly allowed by § 108, it may still be permitted under the fair use doctrine.[29] However, the privi-

---

26 *Id.* With regard to what qualifies as "such aggregate quantities as to substitute for a subscription to or purchase of such work," Congress looked to guidelines formulated by the National Commission on New Technological Uses of Copyrighted Works (CONTU) in consultation with representatives of library associations, publishers, and authors. The guidelines indicate, for example, that six or more copies of an article or articles from a given periodical within five years of a particular request constitute "aggregate quantities as to substitute. . . ." H.R. Rep. No. 94-1733 at 72-73 (1976). The CONTU guidelines are incorporated in the Conference Committee Report accompanying the 1976 Copyright Act. The committee cautioned, however, that the guidelines were not "explicit rules" governing all cases, but merely guidance in the "most commonly encountered interlibrary photocopying situations." It went on to observe that the guidelines "deal with an evolving situation that will undoubtedly require their continuous reevaluation and adjustment." *Id.* at 71.

27 § 108(h). Laura Gasaway posits that as the library's purpose for reproduction, distribution, performance, or display is not limited to preservation but includes scholarship or research, this section can "presumably . . . serve as a collection building section" for works that meet its requirements. Laura N. Gasaway, "America's Cultural Record: A Thing of the Past?" *Houston Law Review* (40): 643, 661 (2003).

28 "Preservation of Orphan Works Act," Title IV of the Family Entertainment and Copyright Act of 2005, Pub. L. No. 109-9, 119 Stat. 226-27 (2005).

29 According to the House Report accompanying the 1976 Copyright Act, even though musical works are excluded from some of the specific privileges in § 108, fair use remains available with respect to such works: "In the case of music, for example, it would be fair use for a scholar doing musicological research to have a library supply a copy of a portion of a score or to reproduce portions of a phonorecord of a work." *House Report*, above note 21, at 78.

leges under § 108 do not supersede any contractual obligations a library may have with respect to a work that it wishes to copy (e.g., under a subscription or donor agreement).[30]

2.4.3 The First Sale Doctrine: § 109

The "first sale doctrine" provides that the owner of a particular copy of a copyrighted work that was lawfully made may transfer or otherwise dispose of that copy. The doctrine prevents the copyright owner from controlling the disposition of a particular copy of a work after the initial sale or transfer of that copy.[31] The first sale doctrine enables, for example, library lending of books, CDs, and DVDs acquired by the library as well as markets in used books and other works.

So far, neither the courts nor the Copyright Office has endorsed broadening the first sale doctrine to allow users to retransmit digital copies over the Internet (sometimes referred to as a "digital first sale doctrine").[32]

2.4.4 Distance Education: § 110(2)

Section 110(2) of the Copyright Act permits certain performances and displays of copyrighted works in the course of instructional transmissions. Section 110(2) was amended by the Technology, Education, and Copyright Harmonization Act (TEACH Act) in 2002 to facilitate distance education, but the authorization it provides to transmit copyrighted materials is carefully circumscribed. For example, only "a government body or an accredited nonprofit educational institution" may invoke the exemption. The performance or display must be made "by, at the direction of, or under the actual supervision of an instructor as an integral part of a class session," offered as part of "systematic mediated instructional activities,"[33] and must be relevant and material to the content of the course. The transmission must be directed to students officially enrolled in the course for which it was made or to officers or employees of governmental bodies as part of their duties. There are additional conditions as well, including provisions related to the security of the copyrighted materials.

---

[30] § 108(f)(4).

[31] § 109(a). There are exceptions for computer programs and sound recordings, designed to deter the development of a commercial rental market, although lending by nonprofit libraries or educational institutions is permitted. § 109(b).

[32] In its *DMCA Section 104 Report*, above note 13, the Copyright Office rejected the argument that receipt of a copy by digital transmission should be treated in the same way as is receipt of a physical copy, with the recipient free to dispose of the digital copy at will. Digital transmission involves making, not merely transferring, a copy. The report expressed concern that application of the first sale doctrine would require deleting the sender's copy when it was sent to the recipient, a feature not generally available on software currently in use and unlikely to be done on a systematic basis by users. The office also rejected the assumption that forward-and-delete is completely analogous to transferring a physical copy, because delivery and return of a digital copy can be done almost instantaneously, so fewer copies can satisfy the same demand. *Id.* at 96-101.

Even downloading a copy onto a disc to give away, at the same time erasing it from one's hard drive, is technically not permitted by the first sale doctrine since it involves creating a copy. It might, however, be considered fair use.

[33] § 110(2)(A).

The distance-education provision of the Copyright Act would permit a library to transmit performances of sound recordings, but only as part of systematic, mediated instructional activities that otherwise qualify for the exemption.

2.4.5 Ephemeral Copying: § 112

Section 112 of the Copyright Act allows certain "ephemeral" or temporary copies to facilitate authorized transmissions (e.g., radio broadcasts) of copyrighted works and for archival purposes. The conditions under which these copies may be made and retained vary according to the nature of the transmitter and the transmission. Specifically, § 112(a) allows an organization licensed or otherwise entitled to transmit a public performance or display of a work (other than a motion picture or audiovisual work) to make no more than one copy of a particular transmission program embodying the performance or display, solely for its own use (e.g., in preparing the work for broadcast) or for archival preservation. No further copies may be made from the copy, and it must be destroyed within six months unless preserved exclusively for archival purposes. Thus, for example, an analog transmission of copyright-protected sound recordings is not covered by the performance right in sound recordings. So, as long as the transmitting organization gets a license to perform the underlying works (for musical recordings, that would likely mean a license from one or more of the performing rights societies[34]—ASCAP, BMI, and/or SESAC—discussed below in section 2.5, "Musical Works"), it may make an ephemeral recording of a transmission program embodying those works under § 112(a).

Other provisions of § 112 provide ephemeral recording privileges in connection with religious broadcasts, transmissions in connection with distance education pursuant to § 110(2), discussed above, and broadcasts directed to the handicapped. Section 112(e) authorizes ephemeral recordings of, among other things, Internet webcasts of sound recordings made pursuant to the compulsory license available for certain digital audio transmissions of sound recordings, discussed in section 2.6. The rationale for the § 112(e) exception is similar to that for § 112(a): the copies are allowed to facilitate the permitted webcasting. Section 112(e) is discussed in greater detail later in this report.[35]

2.5 Musical Works

Under the Copyright Act, the "author" is the initial owner of copyright in a work. In the case of musical compositions, the authors are usually the composer and lyricist (if any)—collectively, the "writers." Writers usually enter into contracts with music publishers, transfer-

---

[34] A "performing rights society" is defined in the Copyright Act as "an association, corporation, or other entity that licenses the public performance of nondramatic musical works on behalf of the copyright owners of such works, such as the American Society of Composers, Authors and Publishers (ASCAP), Broadcast Music, Inc. (BMI), and SESAC, Inc." § 101.

[35] See section 4.3.2, "Webcasting."

ring their copyrights to the publisher in exchange for stated royalties. (Music publishers include, for example, major worldwide publishers such as Warner/Chappell Music and EMI Music and independents such as Peermusic Publishing. In addition, some popular performers and writers create and maintain their own music publishing companies.[36]) The publisher then licenses rights to reproduce the work (in sound recordings or sheet music), to combine it with visual content (e.g., as part of the soundtrack of an audiovisual work), and to perform the work publicly. For historical reasons, reproduction rights and performance rights in musical compositions are commonly exercised through separate entities. The music publisher usually controls the reproduction rights (subject to a compulsory license), while non-dramatic performing rights are usually exercised through a performing rights society, generally ASCAP or BMI. This is discussed in more detail below.

2.5.1 Reproduction of Musical Works

Reproduction of musical compositions in copies of sound recordings[37] is governed by a form of compulsory license known as a "mechanical license," which sets the terms and rate at which the copyright owner must be paid.[38] The mechanical license works like this: once a musical composition has been recorded and distributed in the United States with the copyright owner's permission, others may make their own recordings of the composition (by renting a studio, assembling musicians and singers, and so on), without seeking permission from the copyright owner of the musical composition, provided they pay the set rate and otherwise comply with the terms of the law.[39] The mechanical license is available only if the primary purpose of the subsequent user is to distribute phonorecords to the public for private use (e.g., in CDs, on audiotape, or electronically).[40] So, for example, if Josh Groban wanted to record Irving Berlin's composition *White Christmas* for a Christmas album, the Irving Berlin Music Company may not prevent him from doing so, provided Groban's recording company complies with the terms of the mechanical license. (*White Christmas* has already been recorded by Bing

---

[36] Al Kohn and Bob Kohn, *Kohn on Music Licensing*, 86–87 (Aspen Publishers, 3rd ed., 2002).

[37] Technically, copies of sound recordings are referred to as "phonorecords" under the Copyright Act. § 101.

[38] § 115. The statutory rate is currently 8.5 cents, or 1.65 cents per minute of playing time, whichever is greater. It will go up to 9.1 cents, or 1.75 cents per minute of playing time, whichever is greater, on January 1, 2006. See http://www.copyright.gov/carp/m200a.html.

[39] See § 115. There are, however, limitations on how much the musical composition may be changed. The artist may make a musical arrangement "to the extent necessary to conform it to the style or manner of interpretation of the performance involved," but the arrangement may not "change the basic melody or fundamental character" of the musical composition. Moreover, the arrangement may not be protected as a derivative work under the Copyright Act without the express consent of the copyright owner. § 115(a)(2).

[40] Thus, for example, reproductions of musical compositions on recordings made by background-music services such as Muzak are not covered by the mechanical license and must be negotiated, as those services are not making and distributing phonorecords to the public for personal use.

Crosby with the authorization of the copyright owner—see example 1—and by many others.) The mechanical license does not apply to musical compositions that have never been distributed in phonorecords (e.g., that are unpublished or that have been distributed only in sheet music).

A mechanical license is also available to someone who wishes to duplicate and distribute an existing sound recording, rather than create a new one. However, there are two significant further conditions. First, the existing sound recording must have been lawfully made (and not be, for example, a bootleg copy). Second, permission of the right holder in the sound recording must be obtained.[41] This will entail licensing the sound recording at a negotiated rate, as there is no mechanical license for reproduction and distribution of sound recordings. So, for example, someone who wanted to make and distribute phonorecords of Madonna's rendition of *Like a Virgin* (see example 6, above) as part of a series of "Great Songs of the 1980s" would first have to negotiate a license to reproduce the sound recording with the recording company that owns the rights. If the requestor obtained the license, he or she would then be entitled to a mechanical license (under the terms of the statute) to reproduce the underlying musical composition by Steinberg and Kelly.

In 1995, Congress amended the mechanical license provisions of the copyright law to embrace "digital phonorecord deliveries," that is, phonorecords delivered by means of digital transmission. The mechanical license now allows distribution of the musical composition not only in a phonorecord distributed in a physical format, such as a CD or audio DVD, but also by means of a digital delivery.

Because the requirements of the mechanical compulsory license can be burdensome (e.g., it requires a monthly accounting to copyright owners), reproduction of musical works in phonorecords is usually done pursuant to agreement. The statutory rate (see note 38) effectively acts as a "cap" on license fees; lower rates are often negotiated. Copyright owners of musical compositions are commonly represented by the Harry Fox Agency, an affiliate of the National Music Publishers Association. The Harry Fox Agency is not the only such agency, but it is the largest and best known. Many music publishers have authorized the Harry Fox Agency to license reproduction on their behalf to record companies and others. So, for example, if Josh Groban wished to record *White Christmas*, as a practical matter it would be done pursuant to an agreement between his recording

---

[41] § 115 (a)(1). For recordings fixed before February 15, 1972, the right holder is the person who fixed the sound recording with an express license from the owner of copyright in the musical composition, or under a valid compulsory license. § 115(a)(1)(ii). Since the sound recording is a separate work, permission would have to be sought from the right holder in any event, but the effect of this provision is that if the sound recording right holder assents and all other conditions for the mechanical license are met, the copyright owner of the musical composition cannot deny permission to reproduce the composition as embodied in the sound recording. See Nimmer, above note 10, § 8.04[E][2] at 8-66.2 to 8-66.3. This provision is a partial codification of *Dutchess Music Corp. v. Stern*, 458 F.2d 1305 (9th Cir.), *cert. denied*, 409 U.S. 847 (1972) and related cases decided under the 1909 Act. See discussion in Nimmer, above note 10, at § 8.04[E][1], and § 8.04[E][2] at 8-64 to -66.3.

company and the Harry Fox Agency on behalf of the Irving Berlin Music Company.

2.5.2 Public Performance of Musical Works

Public performance rights are a very important aspect of copyright in a musical composition. It is difficult for independent songwriters, composers, or music publishers to police the unauthorized performance of their works. Consequently, long ago, songwriters and publishers created associations—performing rights societies—to license public performance rights in their musical compositions and to police unauthorized performances. The principal performing rights societies in the United States today are ASCAP, BMI, and SESAC. Each society licenses, generally for a blanket annual fee, the nondramatic performing rights ("small rights") in all the musical compositions in its repertoire through a bulk, or collective, license. The societies' repertoires differ. The licensees of the performing rights societies are individuals and organizations that perform musical compositions (including webcasters, television and radio stations, orchestras, theme parks, stores, and restaurants, among others). The royalties that the performing rights societies receive are split 50–50 between the writers and the publishers and then distributed in proportion to the actual performance of the works, determined on the basis of monitoring, and in some cases of sampling, public performances of music. It is possible to get a performing rights license directly from the copyright owner (usually the music publisher), since the performing rights societies hold only nonexclusive rights, but it is usually more efficient to go through the performing rights societies.[42]

Dramatic performing rights ("grand rights"), such as the use of musical compositions in the performance of plays or operas, as well as the right to reproduce musical compositions on the soundtracks of audiovisual works (known as "synchronization rights"), must be obtained from the music publisher.

2.6 Sound Recordings

The nature of legal protection for sound recordings varies according to the date on which the sound recording was first fixed.

2.6.1 Sound Recordings Fixed on or after February 15, 1972

Federal copyright law did not protect sound recordings until February 15, 1972. All sound recordings fixed, or recorded, on or after that

---

[42] The "jukebox" compulsory license included as § 116 of the Copyright Act of 1976 has since been repealed and replaced with a new § 116 governing "Negotiated licenses for public performances by means of coin-operated phonorecord players." A "coin-operated phonorecord player" is a "machine or device . . . employed solely for the performance of nondramatic musical works by means of phonorecords being activated by the insertion of coins, currency, tokens or other monetary units or their equivalent. . . . " A computer server would not qualify as a "coin-operated phonorecord player," since it is not employed solely to perform nondramatic musical works, nor is it triggered by coins, currency or the like. Moreover, other aspects of § 116 make clear that it governs on-premises performances. In other words, the "jukebox" provisions of the Copyright Act have no relevance to Internet streaming.

date are eligible for federal copyright protection.[43] Madonna's sound recording of *Like a Virgin* (example 6) is protected by federal copyright law, as is the underlying musical composition.

2.6.2 Sound Recordings Fixed prior to February 15, 1972

Sound recordings fixed prior to February 15, 1972, remain eligible for state law protection. Many states protect pre-1972 sound recordings through criminal record piracy statutes, common law protection (against unfair competition, misappropriation, or infringement of common law copyright), or both.[44] When Congress created a unitary federal system of copyright in the 1976 Copyright Act and abolished state common law copyright, it nevertheless carved out pre-1972 sound recordings, leaving them eligible for state law protection.[45] The Copyright Act provides:

> With respect to sound recordings fixed before February 15, 1972, any rights or remedies under the common law or statutes of any State shall not be annulled or limited by [Title 17, which includes federal copyright law] until February 15, 2067.[46]

The sound recordings in example 1 (Bing Crosby/*White Christmas*), example 2 (New York Philharmonic/Mahler), and example 3 (Robert Frost/Frost poems) are all protected by state laws but not by federal copyright law. In the case of the New York Philharmonic's Mahler recording, the underlying work is in the public domain. Example 5 (Casals/Bach) is also protected by state law and will be discussed separately below.

The definition of "sound recording" specifically excludes "the sounds accompanying a motion picture or other audiovisual work."[47] Thus, soundtracks are treated with, and enjoy the same rights as, the motion picture or other audiovisual work of which they

---

43 The Sound Recording Amendment, Pub. L. No. 92-140, § 3, 85 Stat. 391 (1971), passed on Oct. 15, 1971, granted copyright protection to sound recordings fixed on or after its effective date, which was four months later, on February 15, 1972.

44 Nimmer states that "[t]he laws of almost every state render record piracy a criminal offense," but does not canvass the states. Nimmer, above note 10, § 8C.03 at 8C-9.

45 Prior to the effective date of the 1976 Copyright Act, there were two systems of copyright in the country. State law protected unpublished works, and federal law protected published works if the putative copyright owner met the statutory requirements, such as affixing notice. If a work was published without meeting those requirements, it lost state law protection but was not eligible for federal protection, and so fell into the public domain. In *Goldstein v. California*, 412 U.S. 546 (1973), the Supreme Court held that California's protection for pre-1972 sound recordings was not preempted by federal copyright law or the Constitution, regardless of whether those recordings were published or unpublished. In other words, the court concluded that Congress had left the states free to act in this area.

46 § 301(c).

47 *Id.* § 101. Correspondingly, the definition of "motion picture" includes "accompanying sounds, if any." *Id.*

are a part and are not affected by this provision.[48]

There is an exception to the rule that pre-1972 sound recordings are ineligible for federal copyright protection. The Uruguay Round Agreements Act (URAA),[49] passed in 1994, restored copyright in certain *foreign* works that were in the public domain for lack of compliance with U.S. formalities such as copyright notice and renewal. In the case of sound recordings, however, the law did more than merely *restore* copyright: it provided protection for foreign works that would never have been entitled to federal copyright protection, even if they had been published in the United States in the first instance. The law conferred copyright protection on eligible sound recordings of foreign origin fixed before February 15, 1972.[50] Restoration occurred automatically on January 1, 1996, for most works[51] and was not conditioned on any act of the right holder. Restored works are protected for the remainder of the term that they would have been granted if they had not entered the public domain. Thus, at the time of restoration a Mexican sound recording published in 1965 was eligible for protection until 2040;[52] that date was extended by 20 years (i.e., until 2060) by the Copyright Term Extension Act.

To be eligible for restoration of U.S. copyright, a foreign work had to be protected by copyright in its source country on the restoration date (January 1, 1996, for most works). In other words, if such a work had already entered the public domain in its source country by that time, it was not eligible for restoration. In most foreign countries, the term of protection for sound recordings (or "phonograms," as they are commonly called abroad) is 50 years from first publication or fixation. Foreign sound recordings published before 1946 were already in the public domain in their source countries on the restoration date and were not eligible for restoration. Thus, virtually all pre-1946 foreign sound recordings are in the public domain

---

[48] Although the 1909 Copyright Act did not directly address sound recordings, the general understanding prior to the 1976 Copyright Act (and to the 1971 law granting copyright protection to sound recordings) was that the sounds accompanying a motion picture were an integral element of the work and embraced by the copyright in the motion picture. Thus, the exclusion of sounds accompanying a motion picture or other audiovisual work from the definition of "sound recording" in the 1971 law evidenced Congress's opinion that soundtracks were already protected. S. Rep. No. 92-72 at 5 (1971); H.R. Rep. No. 92-487, at 6 (1971); see also Nimmer, above note 10, § 2.09[E][2] at 2-163.

[49] Pub. L. No. 103-465, 108 Stat. 4809 (1994).

[50] *Id*. § 514(a) (discussing the amended 17 U.S.C. § 104A(h)(6)(C)). Eligible sound recordings were those which were not in the public domain in their home country on the date of restoration; had at least one author or right holder who was a national or domiciliary of an eligible country when the work was created, and (if published) were published in an eligible country and not published in the United States within 30 days after foreign publication. Eligible countries include members of the Berne Convention, the World Intellectual Property Organization (WIPO) Copyright Treaty, the WIPO Performances and Phonograms Treaty, and World Trade Organization members that adhere to the Uruguay Round Agreements. *Id*. (discussing 17 U.S.C. § 104A(h)(6)(D)).

[51] This was the date of restoration for works whose source countries were members of the Berne Convention or the World Trade Organization on that date; for other countries, it is the date of adherence. 17 U.S.C. § 104A(h)(2).

[52] The Uruguay Round Agreements Act, Statement of Administrative Action, Pub. Law 103-465, 1994 U.S.C.C.A.N. 4040, 4290.

as far as U.S. federal copyright law is concerned. However, state law protection for these pre-1946 foreign sound recordings may still exist, despite their public domain status under federal copyright law. A New York court recently ruled that sound recordings in the public domain in their source countries can still enjoy protection in New York until the effective date of federal preemption, February 15, 2067.[53] Foreign recordings that were restored to federal copyright protection may be eligible for concurrent state and federal protection, although no case has yet arisen on this question.[54]

The Goldsbrough Orchestra/Telemann recording in example 4, above, was restored to copyright in 1996, since it was still protected by copyright in its source country on that date. (It was protected there until 2002.) Its U.S. copyright protection will last until 2037 (1942 plus 95 years). The Casals/Bach recording in example 5, by contrast, was not restored to federal copyright protection, since it was already in the public domain in the United Kingdom, its source country, on January 1, 1996. It retains state law protection, at least in New York State, until 2067.

For those sound recordings that do enjoy federal copyright protection, including those fixed on or after February 15, 1972, and for earlier foreign sound recordings whose copyrights were restored, the principal rights of concern in this study are the reproduction right and the right of public performance.

2.6.3 Ownership of Rights in Sound Recordings

Rights in sound recordings are generally held by the record companies. There are four major labels (Sony BMG, EMI, Universal Music Group, and Warner Music Group) and thousands of small, independent companies. On policy matters, the major labels and some of the independents work together through a trade association known as the Recording Industry Association of America (RIAA). The labels themselves, not RIAA, license the reproduction of sound recordings. Recently, however, an organization called Sound Exchange was established to represent record companies and performing artists in collecting and distributing royalties from the digital audio transmission of their works. This new organization has a role that is somewhat analogous to that of the Harry Fox Agency and the performing rights societies.

2.6.4 Reproduction of Sound Recordings

Copyright-protected sound recordings enjoy an exclusive reproduction right. The reproduction and distribution of sound recordings,

---

53 See *Capitol Records, Inc. v. Naxos of America, Inc.,* 4 N.Y.3d 540, 561–63 (2005), discussed in section 3.3 of this report.

54 Section 301 of the copyright law, which provides for preemption of state law but preserves state law governing pre-1972 sound recordings until 2067, was not amended to exclude pre-1972 foreign sound recordings whose copyright was restored. Nor did Congress expressly indicate it intended concurrent federal and state protection. See Nimmer, above note 10, § 2.10[B][2].

unlike that of musical compositions, is not subject to a compulsory license.[55]

2.6.5 Public Performance of Sound Recordings

The public performance right in copyright-protected sound recordings is limited to the right "to perform the work publicly by means of a digital audio transmission." The law sets up a three-tiered system of protection for performances of sound recordings.[56] The first tier consists of certain types of public performances that are entirely exempt from the performance right. In other words, such performances may be made with no obligation to the sound recording copyright owner. Exempt activities include live performances, analog transmissions, traditional AM and FM broadcasts, public radio, background-music services, and performances and transmissions in business establishments such as stores and restaurants.[57]

The second tier encompasses digital audio transmissions subject to a compulsory license. The sound recording copyright owner may not prevent these public performances, but the transmitting party must pay royalties to the sound recording copyright owner and performers at the rate set by the Librarian of Congress. Sound Exchange distributes those royalties to recording companies and performers. These performances include subscription digital transmissions (i.e., those limited to paying recipients) and certain eligible nonsubscription digital transmissions. A transmission may be made pursuant to the compulsory license if (1) it is not in the first tier (exempt) category, (2) it is accompanied, if feasible, with the title of the recording, the name of copyright owner, and other information concerning the sound recording and underlying musical work, and (3) the transmitting party meets a number of specific statutory requirements that diminish the risk that the transmissions will be copied or will substitute for having copies (e.g., it does not publish its program in advance, does not play more than a specified number of selections by a particular performer or from a particular phonorecord within a specified time period, and does not seek to evade these conditions by causing receivers to automatically switch program channels).[58]

The third tier consists of certain digital audio transmissions that fall under neither the exemption (first-tier) nor the compulsory license (second-tier) category and thus require negotiating a license with the copyright owner. These are performances perceived to involve a high risk of copying (or of substituting for the sale of copies). They include interactive digital audio services (on-demand streaming) and nonsubscription transmissions that do not meet the condi-

---

[55] There is a limited privilege in § 112, discussed in section 2.4.5 of this report, to make copies to facilitate public performance of sound recordings via broadcast and webcast.

[56] Digital Performance Right in Sound Recordings Act of 1995, Pub. L. No. 104-39, 109 Stat. 336 (1995), as amended by the Digital Millennium Copyright Act of 1998, Pub. L. No. 105-304, 112 Stat. 2860 (1998) (codified in 17 U.S.C. § 114 (2000)).

[57] §§ 106(6), 114(b), (d)(1).

[58] § 114(d)(2).

tions described above because, for example, the transmitting party publishes the program in advance or does not abide by the limitations concerning the number of selections from a particular phonorecord or performer that can be played in a specified time period.[59]

3. State Law Protection for Pre-1972 Sound Recordings

3.1 Overview

To assess issues that might arise under state law in connection with use of pre-1972 sound recordings, we looked at a sampling of five states—California, Illinois, Michigan, New York, and Virginia. We did not do a comprehensive overview of state laws because the National Recording Preservation Board has already commissioned such a study.

Protection for pre-1972 sound recordings in the five states that we surveyed falls under three general categories: (1) criminal record piracy laws; (2) common law rights, variously cast in terms of common law copyright or unfair competition and/or misappropriation, which allow the right holder of a sound recording to stop certain unauthorized uses of the sound recording and recover monetary damages; and (3) in at least one state (California), a civil statute granting ownership rights in sound recordings.[60] We offer here some general observations about state law. The Appendix contains more-detailed discussions of each of our sample states. In addition to record piracy laws, most states have laws against making unauthorized copies of live performances (known as "bootleg" copies). Because this report addresses commercial sound recordings, which were presumably made with authorization, we have not focused on antibootlegging provisions of state law.[61]

3.2 Criminal Statutes

Each of our five sample states had a criminal law prohibiting record piracy. A typical statute is that of Illinois, which provides that a per-

---

[59] §§ 114(d)(2), (3), (4)(A).

[60] There may be other rights as well that pertain to pre-1972 sound recordings (privacy, contract) but generally are not a consideration for *commercial* recordings.

[61] In some cases, unauthorized or "bootleg" recordings of live performances may be the only means of preserving historic performances. The implications of copying and disseminating such recordings—made without the performers' knowledge or approval—is an area that may warrant further study. State laws against copying and distributing bootleg recordings should be included in any comprehensive state law survey. Federal law also protects against making or distributing bootleg recordings. See 17 U.S.C. § 1101 (civil) and 18 U.S.C. § 2319A (criminal). But see *U.S. v. Martignon*, 364 F. Supp. 2d 413 (S.D.N.Y. 2004), appeal pending (2d Cir.) (holding 18 U.S.C. § 2319A unconstitutional) and *Kiss Catalog v. Passport Int'l Prods.*, 350 F.Supp. 2d 823 (C.D. Cal. 2004) (holding § 1101 unconstitutional).

son makes "unlawful use of recorded sounds or images" when he or she:

> Intentionally, knowingly or recklessly transfers or causes to be transferred without the consent of the owner, any sounds or images recorded on any sound or audio visual recording with the purpose of selling or causing to be sold, or using or causing to be used for profit the article to which such sounds or recordings of sound are transferred.[62]

The common elements of these statutes are (1) transfer, or reproduction, of a sound recording; (2) without the consent of the right holder; and (3) with the intent to sell or use for profit (or "commercial advantage" or "private financial gain") the article on which the sound recording has been reproduced. Some state statutes concern only sound recordings; others, such as that of Illinois, extend to sounds and images. It would appear that unauthorized transfer (or copying) to enable public performance (e.g., for Internet streaming) could come within these statutes, but only if done for profit or commercial advantage. Moreover, criminal laws are usually strictly construed according to their terms and thus do not have the ambiguous quality of common law, which is discussed in section 3.3.

Although some states provide explicit exemptions for libraries and archives, they do not always spell out clearly the nature of the exempt activities. In Michigan, for example, there is an exemption for "archival, library or educational purposes."[63] California law has an exemption for not-for-profit educational institutions and government entities that have as their primary purpose "the advancement of the public's knowledge and the dissemination of information regarding America's musical cultural heritage."[64] However, to take advantage of this exemption the entity must make efforts to identify the right holders before reproducing the sound recording, and, if unable to do so at the outset, it must make continuing efforts to do so, by periodically inserting notices in newspapers.

California's exemption raises more questions than it resolves. If California's statute (and other similarly worded statutes) are properly interpreted not to govern activities concerning sound recordings unless those activities are undertaken for commercial advantage or private financial gain, why is it necessary to have a specific exemption for not-for-profit educational institutions and government entities? And if it is necessary to excuse a not-for-profit entity's activities, is that entity at risk in other states without similar exemptions, or in California if it doesn't satisfy the statutory requirements for identifying and notifying right holders?

On the basis of our review of statutes in states other than California, there does not appear to be a significant risk of criminal liability for nonprofit archiving and preservation activity. Nevertheless, a

---

[62] 720 Ill. Comp. Stat. Ann. 5/16-7(a)(1) (2004).

[63] Mich. Comp. Laws Ann. § 752.785(b) (West 2004).

[64] Cal. Penal Code § 653h(h) (2004).

survey of other state laws, as well as further inquiry into the purpose and scope of California's exemption for not-for-profit entities, should be made.

3.3. Common Law

In all states we surveyed except California, civil law protection for sound recordings is exclusively common law, that is, based on judicial decisions rather than statutes. Some states protect pre-1972 sound recordings as part of their unfair competition or misappropriation law. Other states refer to "common law copyright."[65]

Virtually all the cases we found involved a competitor that was reproducing sound recordings without authorization and selling them for profit. Can one conclude that, absent a profit from use of the sound recording, there is no exposure under state common law? Unfair competition law generally requires a commercial benefit to the defendant (though not always direct competition of the parties), so a nonprofit entity that derives no commercial advantage from its preservation and dissemination activities is outside the mainstream. But the language of the cases is not always consistent. Without cases involving nonprofit uses, one cannot say with certainty whether—and under what conditions—such activities would be permitted. This is particularly true in a state that looks to copyright law, rather than to unfair competition law, for guidance.

Common law development results in greater ambiguity (or provides greater flexibility, depending on one's perspective) than exists when rights are defined by statute. As Paul Goldstein explains in his treatise *Copyright*:

> Common law copyright is not a unitary doctrine. The fact that common law copyright is primarily a judge-made doctrine means that it will change over time, and the fact that it is a state law doctrine means that its content will vary from state to state. Further, courts have had little opportunity to flesh out common law copyright's bare bones on such important points as standards for protection, proof of infringement and remedies for infringement.[66]

Similarly, they have had little opportunity to flesh out exceptions.

A recent case clarified the nature of state law rights in pre-1972 sound recordings in New York. *Capitol Records, Inc. v. Naxos of America, Inc.*[67] involved recordings of live performances of classical

---

65 This term is a vestige of the pre-1976 Copyright Act regime under which all unpublished works were protected by common law copyright under state law and most published works were protected, if at all, under federal copyright law. Sound recordings were an exception to this general rule, since even published sound recordings fixed prior to February 15, 1972, could (and still can) be protected under state law.

66 Goldstein, above note 10, § 15.5 at 15:39.

67 372 F.3d 471 (2d Cir. 2004) and 4 N.Y.3d 540 (2005).

music by Pablo Casals, Yehudi Menuhin, and Edwin Fischer, made in the 1930s. (Example 5, above, was taken from the facts of this case.) Under a license from EMI Records (the successor to the company that contracted with the artists to record their performances), Capitol reissued the recordings. Naxos independently obtained and restored the recordings, and began marketing them. Capitol brought suit in federal court under New York law for unfair competition, misappropriation, and common law copyright infringement. The district court granted summary judgment in favor of Naxos—in part because the works were in the public domain in England, where they were originally recorded—and Capitol appealed.

The United States Court of Appeals for the Second Circuit concluded that New York law was unclear in several areas critical to Capitol's claim against Naxos.[68] It sought guidance from the New York Court of Appeals (the highest court in New York State) by "certifying" the principal state law questions in the lawsuit to the New York Court, including the following:

> Does the expiration of the term of a copyright in the country of origin terminate a common law copyright in New York?

> Does a cause of action for common law copyright infringement include some or all of the elements of unfair competition?

> Is a claim of common law copyright infringement defeated by a defendant's showing that the plaintiff's work has slight if any current market value and the defendant's work, although using components of the plaintiff's work, is fairly to be regarded as a 'new product'?[69]

As the Second Circuit explained, "The advent of modern technology to produce digitally enhanced reproductions of historic sound recordings makes it likely that a decision by the Court of Appeals will be important for this emerging field."[70]

The New York Court of Appeals ruled in April 2005. It held that New York law protected the recordings, regardless of whether they were in the public domain in England.[71] In its decision, the court also clarified the nature of common law copyright in New York. A claim for common law copyright, it explained, "consists of two elements: (1) the existence of a valid copyright; and (2) unauthorized reproduction of the work protected by copyright." The court made clear that

---

[68] The term of protection in the United Kingdom for sound recordings was 50 years, so the U.K. copyrights expired in the 1980s. Thus, the works were ineligible for copyright restoration under the URAA. 372 F.3d at 479.

[69] Id. at 484-85.

[70] Id. at 484. Note that a foreign sound recording that is in the public domain in its source country may still be protected under federal copyright law. A foreign work was restored to federal copyright protection if it was still protected in its source country on the restoration date, January 1, 1996, and met other requirements for restoration (see above note 50). It received the full term of U.S. copyright protection, regardless of whether it subsequently fell into the public domain in its source country.

[71] 4 N.Y.3d at 561-63.

bad faith is not an element of a common law infringement claim in New York,[72] and that:

> Copyright infringement is distinguishable from unfair competition, which in addition to unauthorized copying and distribution requires competition in the marketplace or similar actions designed for commercial benefit.[73]

On the final question certified by the Second Circuit, the New York court held that the size of the market or the popularity of a product does not affect the ability to enforce a state law copyright claim. The court observed, with reference to federal copyright law, that Naxos's recordings were not independent creations and that under the fair use doctrine, reproduction of an entire work is generally infringing.[74] It ruled that even if Naxos created a "new product" through remastering, that product could still infringe Capitol's copyright "to the extent that it utilizes the original elements of the protected performances."[75]

3.4 California's Civil Statute

California has a civil statute that provides that the author of a sound recording fixed prior to February 15, 1972, has "an exclusive ownership" interest in that sound recording until February 15, 2047, enforceable except as against anyone who independently creates a similar sound recording.[76] The statute neither specifies the contours of this "exclusive ownership" right nor defines who qualifies as an "author." Both of these issues are left to be developed through case law. Cases brought under the statute to date have involved commercial uses.

3.5 Summary Concerning State Law Protection

How are pre-1972 sound recordings more or less protected than post-1972 sound recordings are? For one thing, the term of protection may not be limited by the date on which the sound recording was fixed or published, or on the basis of the life span of an individual. State law protection can last until 2067, at which time federal law preempts all state law protection for sound recordings. (In California, it lasts only until 2047 by state statute.) Second, the scope of protection can differ. The criminal laws that apply to unauthorized duplication of sound recordings are similar in some respects to those that apply to criminal copyright infringement. But where civil liability is concerned, it is difficult to generalize. State courts may look to federal copyright law in defining the contours of state law protection. Although Goldstein,

---

72 Id. at 563.

73 Id. (citations omitted).

74 Id. at 564.

75 Id. at 564-65.

76 Cal. Civ. Code § 980(a)(2) (2004).

in the treatise cited above, observes that courts in common law cases "frequently consult counterpart provisions in the Copyright Act to fill in doctrinal interstices,"[77] there are so few cases involving educational uses of common law copyrights that it is difficult to draw any conclusions about the nature of the exceptions that a state law court would apply, especially to a published work (as common law copyright traditionally related to unpublished works). State law will not necessarily recognize exceptions within the Copyright Act, but at the same time, if the state law right is strictly limited to an "unfair competition" claim, the conduct excused by federal law may not come within the scope of the state claim in the first instance.

Significant questions remain, and the answers may differ from state to state. For example, do common law claims invariably require commercial gain in the form of profit, or is it enough that the unauthorized use obviates costs that would otherwise have to be incurred (in particular, the expenses involved in licensing sound recordings)? Even if there is no commercial gain on the part of the user, can a claim be brought against an entity whose activities result in commercial harm to the right holder? Does the copyright status of the underlying work affect state law protection for the sound recording?

As discussed above, the New York Court of Appeals recently ruled that common law copyright governs pre-1972 sound recordings, and the court referred to federal law in discussing the scope of that right. While this decision may be persuasive to courts in other states, it is not binding on them. A full survey of state law is desirable. While it is unlikely to bring complete clarity to this murky area, it should put the issues in sharper focus. Even if the survey cannot provide a road map to determining whether or where to clear rights, it may be useful in informing and supporting a decision to seek legislation to fulfill the preservation mission of archives and libraries.

4. Digital Preservation and Dissemination of Sound Recordings

Sections 4.1–4.3 of this report address in detail library preservation and dissemination activities with respect to copyright-protected works (including pre-1972 sound recordings restored to copyright protection, post-1972 sound recordings, and any musical, literary, or other works that underlie sound recordings and have not yet entered the public domain). Although pre-1972 U.S. sound recordings are not copyright protected, the scope of federal copyright law can be relevant to state law protection, as discussed above. Section 4.4 focuses on the possible effect of fair use and equitable doctrines. Section 4.5 focuses on sound recordings that have no protection under federal law, discussing permissible activities with respect to those recordings as compared with such activities with respect to copyrighted works.

---

[77] Goldstein, above note 10, § 15.5 at 15:39.

4.1 Digital Preservation and Replacement Copies: Copyright-Protected Works

As discussed in section 2.4.2, a qualifying library or archives may make up to three copies of an unpublished work in its collection for preservation and security or for deposit and research use at another library. A library may also make up to three copies of a published work to replace one that is damaged, deteriorating, lost, or stolen, or whose format has become obsolete, if the library determines, after "reasonable effort," that an unused original cannot be obtained at a fair price. The copies may be in digital form, but a digital copy made pursuant to these provisions may not be made available outside the library premises.

The scope of these provisions is unclear in many respects, and there has been little litigation to provide guidance. Some of the ambiguities are discussed below.

4.1.1 What Is a "Reasonable" Effort?

The privilege in § 108(c) is contingent on a library determining "after reasonable effort . . . that an unused replacement cannot be obtained at a fair price." Other library privileges require similar "due diligence" efforts. For example, the special-use privilege for the last 20 years of copyright requires a library first to undertake "a reasonable investigation" to determine whether the work is subject to normal exploitation and cannot be obtained at a fair price. The definition of "obsolete," as discussed in section 4.1.2 below, similarly depends on an inquiry into whether playback equipment is "reasonably available." The statute does not define what is "reasonable." The legislative history of the 1976 Copyright Act does, however, shed some light on it:

> The scope and nature of a reasonable investigation to determine that an unused replacement cannot be obtained will vary according to the circumstances of a particular situation. It will always require recourse to commonly-known trade sources in the United States, and in the normal situation also to the publisher or other copyright owner (if such owner can be located at the address listed in the copyright registration), or an authorized reproducing service.[78]

The sources to which one would refer will vary with the particular type of work. At the current time, a "reasonable" investigation for a phonorecord presumably would also entail use of Internet search tools to identify Web and other retailers as well as any sources through which a knowledgeable purchaser would seek an unused replacement of the same work, in the same or a newer format that is commercially available.

---

[78] *House Report*, above note 21, at 75-76. There is little legislative history for § 108(h); presumably this language is relevant also to the "reasonable investigation" standard of that provision.

4.1.2 When Is an Existing Format "Obsolete"?

The adjective "obsolete" means that the machine or device needed to "render perceptible a work stored in that format" is "no longer manufactured or is no longer reasonably available in the commercial marketplace."[79] In other words, if playback equipment is readily available in the marketplace, the format is not "obsolete." Because turntables remain available, under the current formulation of the law, long-play record albums (LPs), and even 78-rpm discs, are not in an obsolete format. In a recent rule-making proceeding, the Copyright Office concluded that this provision does not allow "preemptive archival activity to preserve works before they become obsolete."[80] It is permissible to copy individual recordings that are damaged or deteriorating; however, the law does not define "deteriorating."

4.1.3 May Libraries Rely on Others to Make Digital Copies?

If a library has a right to make a digital copy pursuant to § 108, may it rely on another library to make the copy? The terms of § 108(c) suggest that the privilege to copy published works belongs to the library with the damaged, deteriorating, lost, or stolen copy. In contrast, section 108(b), which relates to copying of unpublished works, specifically allows a library to make a copy for another library. Nevertheless, insisting that the library with the privilege to make and retain a copy of a published work must itself undertake the reproduction process seems like an overly technical reading that does not comport with common sense. A library whose copy of a particular work is lost or stolen would presumably have to make a copy from that of another library. The second library may understandably prefer to make a copy for the first library, rather than to yield control of its copy of the work and deprive its patrons of access while it ships the work to the first library and awaits its return. Even if not permitted by the strict terms of § 108, fair use would likely permit one library to make a replacement copy for another library, provided that the recipient library met the conditions for making a copy itself and that all aspects of the arrangement were nonprofit and noncommercial, and otherwise in compliance with the law.

Whether a commercial entity may make preservation copies on behalf of a library or an archives is a different question. Libraries sometimes contract out replacement copying (e.g., transferring works to microform or restoring film) for convenience, or because of the particular expertise provided by outside contractors. However, a third-party commercial contractor does not necessarily "stand in the shoes" of the party with a legal privilege.[81] We are not aware of

---

[79] § 108(c)(2).

[80] Recommendation of the Register of Copyrights in RM 2002-4; Rulemaking on Exemptions from the Prohibition on Circumvention of Copyright Protection Systems for Access Control Technologies (October 27, 2003) at 63, http://www.copyright.gov/1201/docs/registers-recommendation.pdf.

[81] See, for example, *Princeton University Press v. Michigan Document Services, Inc.*, 99 F.3d 1381, 1386 & n.2 (6th Cir. 1996) (en banc), *cert. denied*, 117 S. Ct. 1336 (1997). See also note 21, above.

any claims made against libraries or third-party contractors with respect to these activities. It is possible that the outsourcing that has occurred to date has been limited in nature and scope, has had little if any economic impact on copyright owners, and therefore has not raised concerns. However, if the right holder were to object (e.g., where a third party is digitizing replacement material for a library when the copyright owner itself is preparing or planning to prepare a digital version of the work), it is important to bear in mind that there is no specific authorization for this third-party activity in the law. (Whether it is permissible would depend on the nature and scope of the third-party activities.)

4.1.4 Are Collaborative Digital Preservation Projects Permissible?

Collaborative preservation projects can avoid the need for different institutions to engage in duplicative work and can maximize the use of sometimes-strained library resources. Section 108(g), however, poses a potential obstacle to collaboration projects. Section 108(g)(1) states that the rights of reproduction and distribution provided to libraries under § 108 extend to the "isolated and unrelated reproduction or distribution of a single copy or phonorecord of the same material on separate occasions," but not to "the related or concerted reproduction or distribution of multiple copies or phonorecords of the same material, whether made on one occasion or over a period of time. . . ."

This provision appears to be directed more to the photocopying and distribution privileges set forth elsewhere in § 108 than to library preservation activities, and to reflect a concern that copies made by libraries should not substitute for a purchase or subscription to a work.[82] In the case of preservation or replacement copies made pursuant to § 108(b) or (c), this is not an issue. Unpublished works will not be available for purchase or subscription, and copies of published works may be made only if an unused replacement cannot be obtained at a fair price. These considerations are not, however, reflected in the terms of § 108(g).

Accordingly, there is no simple, yes-or-no answer to whether collaborative digital preservation projects are permissible. Not all aspects of preservation programs involve copying: libraries can pool their resources to investigate such questions as the copyright status of a work and whether it is currently available on the market or subject to commercial exploitation,[83] or to create databases with information concerning works maintained in digital form that can serve

---

[82] See *House Report*, above note 21, at 75: "[S]ection 108 would not excuse reproduction or distribution . . . if the photocopying activities were 'systematic' in the sense that their aim was to substitute for subscriptions or purchases." This concern is made explicit in § 108(g)(2), which preserves libraries' right to participate in interlibrary arrangements, provided they do not receive copies for distribution "in such aggregate quantities as to substitute for a subscription or purchase" of a work.

[83] The permissibility of copying a work may change over time. For example, it may become commercially available.

as resources for libraries whose copies of those works have been lost or stolen, or have otherwise become unavailable. Such cooperation has existed with respect to analog preservation and replacement activities (in the form of master microform registries), and it is now beginning to develop in connection with digitized works. Moreover, § 108 does not represent the outer bounds of permissible library activities, so even if § 108(g) were read to limit the library privileges to noncollaborative activities, fair use is still available.[84] Presumably, fair use would allow some collaboration projects among libraries to digitize works, but such projects would have to be evaluated on a case-by-case basis and carefully managed to ensure, for example, that no participant came away with material that it was not entitled to make for itself.[85] The scope of dissemination would also be very relevant to a fair use determination.

4.1.5 Use of Digital Preservation and Replacement Copies

The statute states that digital copies made pursuant to § 108(b) and (c) may not be made available to the public in digital format "outside the premises" of the library. It does not, however, define the word *premises*. The legislative history indicates that the references to "the 'premises of the library or archives' in amended § 108(b)(2) and (c) mean only physical premises" and do not refer to online digital libraries "that exist only in the virtual (rather than physical) sense . . . ."[86] Typical definitions of the word *premises* are as follows: (a) a tract of land with the buildings thereon, and (b) a building or part of a building [usually] with its appurtenances [as grounds].[87]

This suggests that the privilege would be limited to buildings owned or controlled by that library.

4.2 Special-Use Privileges under § 108(h): Copyright-Protected Works

Section 108(h) of the Copyright Act allows a library, archives, or nonprofit educational institution to make and use copies of copyright-protected works in the last 20 years of their term. It allows broader use of the copies made than do § 108(b) or (c), but an institution must meet several conditions to trigger the privilege.

If it meets the conditions of § 108(h), the authorized institution may "reproduce, distribute, perform or display a copy of the work"

---

[84] § 108(f)(4). See Gasaway, above note 27, at 653.

[85] This would not be an easy task. Careful management would have to be undertaken to ensure that such projects did not improperly become a collection-building mechanism for libraries, or that changing circumstances did not affect the permissibility of making digital copies. A work might become commercially available, for example, eliminating the justification for making replacement copies, or subject to commercial exploitation and therefore not available for use under § 108(h).

[86] Committee Print of the House of Representatives Committee on the Judiciary: House Comm. On the Judiciary, 105th Cong., 2d Sess., Section-by-Section Analysis of H.R. 2281 As Passed by the United States House of Representatives on August 4, 1998, at 48–49 (1998) [hereinafter, *House Manager's Report*].

[87] *Webster's Ninth New Collegiate Dictionary* (Merriam-Webster 1985).

in pursuit of preservation, scholarship, or research objectives. Thus, a library is authorized to perform or display a copy made under this provision (in contrast to § 108(b) or (c)), and there appears to be no restriction on distributing these copies to other libraries for collection-building purposes.

To qualify for these expanded-use rights, the institution must undertake a "reasonable investigation" to determine whether the work is subject to normal commercial exploitation or available at a "fair price." It must also check with the Copyright Office to see whether the copyright owner has filed any notices to that effect. The availability inquiry under § 108(h), unlike that of § 108(c), is not limited to unused copies.[88]

4.3 Dissemination via Internet Streaming: Copyright-Protected Works

May libraries and archives stream copyright-protected sound recordings over the Internet? We will consider here two forms of Internet streaming that a library or an archives might engage in: (1) on-demand, interactive streaming services in which users can individually request to have specific sound recordings streamed to them; and (2) noninteractive streaming, or "webcasting," where the webcaster, not the users, determines the sound recordings that are streamed, and multiple users can access the stream. The term *webcasting* is used differently by different people. In some cases, it refers to any streaming over the Internet;[89] in others, it refers more specifically to noninteractive, nonsubscription audio transmissions.[90] We use the term in the latter sense and assume that any webcasting that a library would do

---

[88] No case has directly addressed whether a sound recording may be copied under § 108(h) when the underlying work is protected by copyright and not in the last 20 years of its term. However, in *Russell v. Price*, 612 F.2d 1123 (9th Cir. 1979), the court held that copyright owners of George Bernard Shaw's play *Pygmalion*, which was still covered by copyright, could prevent distribution of the film version of the play, even though the film had fallen into the public domain, *id*. at 1128. Similarly, in *Filmvideo Releasing Corp. v. Hastings*, 668 F.2d 91 (2d Cir. 1981), the court held that even though films based on the Hopalong Cassidy stories had fallen into the public domain, a license for television exhibition had to be obtained from the owners of the copyrights in the underlying books, which were still protected by copyright, *id*. at 92. Of course, § 108(h) provides only a limited privilege and may not deprive copyright owners of the underlying work of economic rights in the same way that a contrary result in the cases discussed above might have done. On the other hand, the structure of § 108(h) clearly demonstrates Congressional concern that the expanded privileges should not harm the economic interests of copyright owners whose works may be subject to this privilege, and the copyright owner of a protected work still subject to commercial exploitation could be adversely affected by broad use under § 108(h) of a sound recording embodying that work.

[89] *Bonneville Int'l Corp. v. Peters*, 347 F.3d 485, 489 (3d Cir. 2003) ("This real-time transmission of sound recordings over the Internet is known as 'streaming' and 'webcasting,' and the transmitter of an Internet stream of music is known as a 'webcaster.'") (footnote omitted).

[90] *House Manager's Report*, above note 86, at 50 ("the digital sound recording performance right applies to nonsubscription digital audio services such as webcasting. . . ."); U.S. Copyright Office, Public Performance of Sound Recordings: Definition of a Service, 65 Fed. Reg. 77292, 77296 (December 11, 2000) ("noninteractive nonsubscription service[s] streaming music over the Internet" are "now known in the industry as webcasters. . . .").

would meet the requirements for the compulsory license of performance rights in sound recordings (for example, not only the recordings transmitted but also their order would be determined by the library, not by end users, and the schedule would not be published in advance).[91] This discussion does not address digital downloads. It assumes that the streaming involved would not result in a complete, usable copy of the streamed work in the end user's computer.

The following discussion of streaming and webcasting sound recordings relates to sound recordings protected by federal copyright law, including U.S. sound recordings created on or after February 15, 1972, and foreign sound recordings whose copyrights were restored. We discuss pre-1972 U.S. sound recordings in section 4.5. State law governs the permissibility of streaming those works. The discussion in this section also relates to copyrighted works underlying sound recordings, regardless of whether or not the sound recordings are protected by federal copyright law.

Streaming (whether or not interactive) involves the following copyright-relevant events. First, a copy of the work to be streamed (for example, a sound recording, including the underlying musical composition) must be made on the server. Streaming usually requires multiple server copies to serve users with different technological capabilities (e.g., different media players, different bandwidths). Second, streaming involves reproductions made in the buffer of the recipients' computers (though the copyright significance of those copies is a matter of debate, as discussed in section 4.3.1, below). Third, streaming involves a public performance of the streamed works.

We consider below the ways in which streaming may implicate copyright rights, whether the proposed streaming activities would fall under any exception or privilege the law grants to libraries and archives, and if it does not, from whom a license would be obtained.

4.3.1 Interactive, On-Demand Streaming
4.3.1.1 Sound Recordings
Public performance. On-demand interactive streaming would be considered a public performance of copyrighted sound recordings and would not be subject to the compulsory license available for certain digital audio transmissions. Systematic, on-demand streaming of copyrighted sound recordings does not fall under any exceptions generally available to libraries and archives.[92] It would require negotiating a license with the copyright owners of the sound recording.

Reproduction onto server to enable streaming. Reproduction onto a server for the purpose of digital streaming to remote users does not appear to fall under a specific library exception. Copies made pursu-

---

[91] A library could take requests without the service being deemed interactive, as long as the requested recording is not transmitted within one hour of the request or at a time designated by the library or the requester. § 114(j)(7). In other words, the greater ability that users have to plan in advance, the more likely the transmission will be deemed interactive.

[92] Narrowly targeted streaming activities would be permissible if they fell under a specific exception, for example, streaming to enrolled students by a qualifying entity as part of systematic mediated instruction that meets the conditions of the distance education exemption in § 110(2), discussed in section 2.4 of this report.

ant to library preservation exceptions under § 108(b) and (c) may not be made available outside library premises. A copy made pursuant to § 108(h) could be placed on a server, but this provision is currently of limited use, since there are virtually no sound recordings in their last 20 years of copyright protection. Finally, § 112(a) allows the creation of an ephemeral copy of a "transmission program" to facilitate a transmission allowed pursuant to an exception to copyright, a compulsory license, or an agreement with the copyright owner. Since public performance by means of an on-demand digital transmission is within the sound recording copyright owner's exclusive rights, there is no right to make a copy under § 112(a) absent an agreement with the copyright owners.[93] For sound recordings of musical compositions, the copyright owner will generally be a recording company. In the case of the Robert Frost recording of Frost poems (example 3, above), the copyright owner of the sound recording may be Frost's publisher or the Frost estate or heirs.

Buffer copies. As discussed above, on-demand streaming would require negotiation of an agreement with the sound recording copyright owners. Any such agreement would presumably embrace buffer copies. The question of whether making those copies is an independent event for copyright purposes is discussed in the next section, in connection with musical works.

4.3.1.2 Musical Compositions

Public performance. Streaming entails a public performance of the musical composition being streamed. Public performance licenses would have to be obtained from the performing rights societies (ASCAP, BMI, SESAC).[94] ASCAP and BMI operate under antitrust consent decrees and cannot deny licenses to users who request them; the only issue is the amount of license fee to be paid.

Reproduction onto server to enable streaming. Reproduction onto a server for the purpose of digital streaming to remote users does not fall under § 108(b) and (c). It may be permissible under § 108(h) during the last 20 years of copyright protection, but the conditions in that provision (see section 2.4) must be met. Even for copyrighted musical compositions that do not qualify for the expanded-use privileges in § 108(h), § 112(a) allows the creation of an ephemeral copy of a transmission program to facilitate a permitted transmission (including performances licensed by the performing rights societies). However, it is doubtful whether on-demand streaming could qualify as a "transmission program," defined as "a body of material that, as an aggregate, has been produced for the sole purpose of transmis-

---

[93] Server copies can be made pursuant to § 112(b) and (f) for transmissions that qualify under the distance education exception in § 110(2). For purposes of this report, it is assumed that activities under § 110(2) are not sufficient to meet the Library's preservation and dissemination mandate, but this area deserves further study.

[94] Such licenses would not, however, encompass playing original cast recordings in their entirety, for that would entail a dramatic performance or "grand" right. E-mail correspondence from I. Fred Koenigsberg, White & Case, General Counsel, ASCAP (November 19, 2004) (copy on file with author).

sion to the public in sequence and as a unit."[95] In any event, § 112(a) would authorize the making of only a single copy, which may be insufficient for streaming purposes.

It is also unclear whether the § 115 compulsory license for musical compositions can be interpreted to encompass the necessary server copies.[96] If not, permission to make additional server copies would have to be sought from music publishers, many of which are represented by the Harry Fox Agency. This is an area where the law is still developing.

Buffer copies. There is a controversy over whether the copy created in the buffer of the recipient's computer in the course of on-demand streaming implicates the reproduction right. The Copyright Office takes the position that although a reproduction may be made, it is merely incidental to the performance and does not, or should not, have independent economic significance. Music publishers dispute this view, pointing to, among other things, the ease with which streams in buffers can be captured and retained, and to the definition in the law of "digital phonorecord delivery," which seems to distinguish between digital phonorecord deliveries in general and those "where the reproduction or distribution of a phonorecord is incidental to the transmission which constitutes the digital phonorecord delivery."[97] This issue is unresolved.

In order to move forward in the face of these legal ambiguities and to enter the on-demand streaming market, the Harry Fox Agency, the National Music Publishers Association, and the RIAA entered into an interim agreement in 2001 that allows on-demand streaming of musical compositions (including the right to make the necessary server and buffer copies) in exchange for payments by the RIAA to the copyright owners of the musical compositions. The agreement also covers "limited downloads" (i.e., downloads limited in terms of time or number of plays). It envisions that payment will be adjusted when the legal ambiguities are resolved and a royalty rate is established. The agreement does not address any webcasting issues.[98]

4.3.1.3 Other Types of Underlying Works
For other types of underlying works, such as literary or dramatic works, the analysis is essentially the same as that for musical works.

Authors of literary works usually enter into contracts with book publishers to license their works for reproduction in various forms. Many book-publishing agreements encompass the right to license audio recordings of the work, but in some cases those rights are re-

---

[95] § 101.

[96] *See generally* Statement of Marybeth Peters, Register of Copyrights, before the Subcommittee on Courts, The Internet and Intellectual Property, House Committee on the Judiciary, 108th Cong., 2d Sess. (March 11, 2004), at http://www.copyright.gov/docs/regstat031104.html [hereinafter, Statement of Marybeth Peters].

[97] § 115 (c)(3). *See* Statement of Marybeth Peters, above note 96; Kohn & Kohn, above note 36, at 1328-32.

[98] The legal conclusions on which the agreement is based are not universally accepted. *See*, for example, Statement of Marybeth Peters, above note 96, at 9–10.

tained by or have reverted to the author or his or her heirs. Frequently, the same party holds the reproduction rights and the performance rights, unlike the case with musical compositions. Nonetheless, it may be more difficult to locate the right holder of a literary work than the right holder of a musical composition because the literary publishing industry has no licensing agencies akin to the Harry Fox Agency, ASCAP, or BMI. Permissions usually have to be sought in the first instance from the publisher. This would be the case for someone seeking to use the Frost poems that underlie the Robert Frost recording in example 3, above.

4.3.2 Webcasting

We turn next to the copyright implications of webcasting (where the particular recordings streamed, and their order, are determined by the webcaster), to consider whether they differ from those of interactive, on-demand streaming.

4.3.2.1 Sound Recordings

Public performance. A compulsory license is available for subscription digital audio transmissions and nonsubscription digital audio transmissions that meet the statutory requirements (for example, the transmission is accompanied, if feasible, by copyright information, and the transmitting party meets a number of specific statutory requirements that diminish the risk that the transmissions will be copied). For example, the transmitting party may not (1) publish its program in advance, (2) play more than a specified number of selections by a particular performer or from a particular phonorecord within a specified time period, or (3) seek to evade these conditions by causing receivers to automatically switch program channels.[99]

Reproduction onto server to enable streaming. Reproduction of sound recordings onto a server for webcasting is covered by the statutory license in § 112(e).[100]

Buffer copies. Buffer copies are apparently regarded as falling within the statutory license.

4.3.2.2 Musical Compositions

The analysis of rights in musical compositions as they relate to webcasting is similar to that for on-demand streaming, although webcasts may be more likely to qualify as "transmission programs." Section 112(e) relates only to sound recordings, not to musical compositions or other underlying works. Apparently, owners of rights in musical compositions have not been asserting claims with respect to buffer copies made in the course of webcasts.[101]

---

[99] § 114(d)(2). Thus, playing the entirety of an original cast album would not be permitted under the statutory license.

[100] § 112(e) authorizes creation of an ephemeral copy of a sound recording transmitted under a § 114(f) statutory license. It allows a single reproduction unless the terms and conditions of the statutory license allow for more.

[101] While these copies may be technologically indistinguishable from buffer copies created in on-demand streaming, they are perceived to be less likely to result in copies that are retained and reused by end users (and thus less threatening to music copyright owners' financial interests).

4.3.2.3 Other Types of Underlying Works
The analysis is similar to that for on-demand streaming.

4.4 Fair Use and Equitable Doctrines

4.4.1 Fair Use

Could streaming of sound recordings qualify as fair use? A comprehensive program to systematically digitize and stream sound recordings over the Internet without regard to their copyright status would have little claim to fair use; however, it is not easy to determine when a more modest program might qualify under fair use. Fair use determinations are fact based, so it is difficult to do anything but make general observations and assumptions about possible digital preservation and dissemination programs.

The first fair-use factor, the purpose and character of the use, favors nonprofit, educational, and scholarly uses. This factor also favors "transformative" uses that analyze, supplement, or otherwise build on, rather than merely reproduce, the original. Transformative use is not essential to fair use, though the first factor usually weighs more heavily in favor of fair use where there is a transformative aspect. The first fair use factor would likely favor library copying and streaming of sound recordings limited to research or scholarly uses.

The second fair use factor, the nature of the copyrighted work, would likely favor copyright owners, as the subject works are predominantly creative rather than factual.

The third factor—amount and substantiality of the portion of the work used in relation to the work as a whole—would also favor copyright owners, if the entire works were used. The assessment of this particular factor could change if only small excerpts were used (especially if the excerpts were not of particularly high quality), but such excerpts may not satisfy the scholarly and research goals of libraries and their patrons.[102]

The fourth factor, which is the effect on the potential market for or value of the copyrighted works, is the hardest to assess. Sound recordings (and underlying musical or other works) vary significantly in their market potential. Digital technology has brought about renewed interest in older works, and rereleasing older sound recordings can be done with a smaller financial investment on the part of copyright owners than previously required. Digital technology may give new life to older works that had little apparent market potential 10 or 15 years ago.

How might widespread use of copyrighted works in a particular manner, without apparent objection by copyright owners, affect a fair use determination? Assume, for example, that it is common practice for libraries to make available 30-second audio clips on the Web, and that copyright owners have raised no objection to this

---

[102] For some users whose goal is simply to identify a particular work and determine its general style or whether it is the same as or different from another work, a short excerpt may be enough. Other users, however, may need to study—and possibly to transcribe—the entire work.

practice.[103] A custom of permitted use (indicating apparent acquiescence by a particular copyright owner or similarly situated copyright owners) can sometimes favor a fair use defense.[104] However, copyright owners' failure to take action with respect to a particular practice does not necessarily indicate that they consent to it. In the early stages of a new technology, enforcement costs that copyright owners would incur may outweigh the likely return from the use, and a practice develops whereby users proceed without permission. Over time, however, copyright owners set up enforcement mechanisms.[105]

Internet streaming is a relatively new technology. It is too early to assume that certain practices (e.g., streaming by libraries or nonprofit institutions, without authorization, of 30 seconds of a sound recording) have become customary or that copyright owners acquiesce in them. These practices do not yet appear to be widespread or generally accepted, and many copyright owners may simply be unaware of them. The owners may also have decided to focus enforcement resources in other areas, such as infringement through file sharing, which is a serious threat to their business. In short, as of this writing, these practices do not appear to be sufficiently established to warrant a conclusion that they are common practices for which copyright owners' acquiescence can be inferred (i.e., de facto fair use).

The availability of a fair use defense cannot be predicted with certainty. As with collaborative preservation projects, some streaming projects might qualify, depending on factors such as the categories of subject works, who will have access to the materials, and under what circumstances. But the structure of the Copyright Act (e.g., the limitations placed on copies made under § 108(b) and (c), and the limitations placed on works streamed pursuant to § 110(2), including the technological protection requirements), lead to the conclusion that fair use could not justify a comprehensive program to digitize copyrighted sound recordings and to make them publicly available over the Internet.[106]

4.4.2 General Equitable Defenses

Can failure to object to certain uses of their works in the past preclude copyright owners from taking action in the future? For example, if record companies fail to prosecute unauthorized uses of sound recordings that are in the public domain in their country of origin but still protected in the United States by common law or federal

---

[103] This premise is included for the sake of discussion. We have no basis at this time for concluding that this is a common practice and we understand that some copyright owners do object to such uses.

[104] Wendy Gordon, *Fair Use as Market Failure: A Structural and Economic Analysis of the Betamax Case and Its Predecessors*, 82 *Colum. L. Rev.* 1600, 1641 (1982).

[105] *Id.* at 1621.

[106] Making copyrighted works available over the Internet to users outside the United States also carries potential risk of liability to foreign right holders under the laws of other countries. What the U.S. courts might deem fair use could be an infringement elsewhere, and courts around the world are not in agreement as to where an infringement on the Internet occurs (e.g., the country of origin, country(ies) where the material is received).

copyright, have they abandoned their rights in the United States?

Right holders can, by their conduct, evidence an intent to give up their copyright—or at least certain rights under their copyright—thereby precluding them from succeeding in an infringement action. There are several relevant equitable defenses to copyright infringement, including abandonment, estoppel, waiver, and laches. There is considerable overlap between these defenses, each of which is described below.[107]

Abandonment. Abandonment of copyright requires an intent to give up copyright rights and an overt act demonstrating that intent.[108] That overt act might be, for example, publication of the work by the author together with an unequivocal statement that the work is "dedicated to the public domain." Failure to prosecute copyright infringement by third parties has not been considered evidence of abandonment by the courts.[109] The application of the abandonment defense was at issue in the *Capitol Records v. Naxos* case discussed above, but the Second Circuit Court ruled there were still factual issues to be determined by the district court.

Estoppel. Estoppel is a legal bar to proceeding on a claim that is inconsistent with the claimant's previous statements or conduct. To establish the defense of estoppel, a defendant must demonstrate that

(1) the party to be estopped (i.e., the right holder) knew the facts of defendant's infringing conduct and did not object;

(2) the right holder intended that his conduct would be relied upon, or act in such a way that the defendant had a right to believe the right holder intended his conduct to be relied upon;

(3) the defendant was ignorant of the true facts; and

(4) the defendant relied on the right holder's conduct to his detriment.[110]

This defense is relevant only as between the right holder and a specific defendant. It requires proof of knowledge of specific infringing activities. One cannot establish waiver with respect to a particular defendant's activities by demonstrating that a right holder knew of infringing activities by a different party and did not object, or that another party relied on the right holder's conduct to his detriment.

Waiver. Similar to estoppel, waiver requires proof of "intentional relinquishment of a known right with both knowledge of its existence and an intention to relinquish it."[111]

Laches. The word *laches* refers to undue delay in asserting legal rights. To establish a laches defense, a defendant would have to

---

[107] Our research on equitable defenses is derived primarily from federal law sources. Although we believe the principles described here would also apply in state court, we have not done a state law survey concerning the requirements to establish these defenses.

[108] *Capitol Records*, 372 F.3d at 483.

[109] *Id.* at 484, citing *Paramount Pictures Corp. v. Carol Publishing Group*, 11 F. Supp. 2d 329, 337 (S.D.N.Y. 1998); Goldstein, above note 10, § 9.3 at 9:12.

[110] Nimmer, above note 10, § 13.07 at 13-280 to -8; Goldstein, above note 10, § 9.5.2 at 9:33-35.

[111] *Capitol Records*, 372 F.3d at 482 (New York law).

prove that a right holder failed to assert his rights in a diligent manner and that the defendant was prejudiced by the reliance on the right holder's inaction. One cannot assert a defense of laches on the basis of a right holder's failure to take action against another party.[112]

In each case, the defense, if proved, is a complete defense to copyright infringement. However, the defenses are very fact-specific, requiring a demonstration of an overt act, in the case of abandonment, or of a knowing relinquishment. Thus, some right holders may by their conduct have given up rights, but others have not. These defenses may be effective in the context of specific infringement suits but do not provide the basis for a comprehensive business strategy.

4.5 Pre-1972 Sound Recordings without Federal Copyright Protection

How does protection for pre-1972 sound recordings that lack federal copyrights differ from the protection described above? Is there greater ability on the part of libraries to make digital copies or to stream those copies?

To the extent that such recordings embody other works (principally musical works), the copyright status of those underlying works must be taken into account. Accordingly, the analysis above with respect to musical and other works that underlie copyrighted sound recordings is applicable as well to pre-1972 sound recordings. But what about the sound recordings themselves?

There is no simple answer to the question whether libraries can copy and stream pre-1972 sound recordings without violating state law. Our preliminary research demonstrates that there is a substantial body of state law that pertains to pre-1972 sound recordings. Laws vary from state to state. Most states appear to have criminal laws concerning sound recordings, and many also have relevant civil laws. Determining the scope of permissible use under state laws—specifically, whether digital preservation copies can be made, and whether they can be streamed to users from library servers—requires a more comprehensive survey of these state laws. What is permissible in one state may be illegal in another.

On the basis of our limited review of state law, we can, however, make some tentative observations:

State criminal laws: Our review suggests that digital preservation and streaming of pre-1972 sound recordings by nonprofit libraries is unlikely to violate state criminal laws. The criminal laws in the states we surveyed generally focus on for-profit distribution of copies of sound recordings, done with intent. Criminal laws are strictly construed according to their terms; for this reason, provided a library does not sell the recordings or use them for profit or commercial advantage, it will not violate these laws, even if its activities result in commercial harm to the right holder. However, the laws of other states may vary from those we reviewed (and California's

---

112 *See generally* Goldstein, above note 10, § 9.5.1 at 9:26–33 (2005 Supp.).

law would bear further investigation, as discussed below). It is essential to do a complete state survey to responsibly assess potential criminal liability.

State civil laws: Most state civil law in this area is common law, developed on a case-by-case basis. Because its contours (e.g., what rights are covered, what exceptions exist) are not strictly defined and are subject to change, it is difficult to assess the risk of civil liability for digital copying and dissemination of pre-1972 sound recordings. The cases we found involved defendants who sought to gain commercially from the use of plaintiffs' sound recordings. But the elastic nature of common law leaves open the possibility that commercial harm to the right holder can be the basis of a claim, even if the user does not derive a commercial benefit. Moreover, a state could rely on federal copyright law for guidance, and commercial benefit is not an essential element of a federal copyright claim. For example, in *Capitol Records v. Naxos*, discussed in section 3.3, the New York Court of Appeals held that marketplace competition or commercial benefit is not essential to a common law copyright claim (as they are to an unfair competition claim), and the court looked to federal law for guidance on the scope of the common law rights.

A survey of state laws will reduce the uncertainty concerning the scope of state law protection and likely suggest ways to minimize the risk of liability in connection with digital preservation and dissemination of pre-1972 sound recordings. But our research suggests that even a detailed survey will not completely resolve these issues. New legislation to establish a library privilege to preserve and appropriately disseminate these materials would be very desirable.

In the meantime, it seems unlikely that activities within the bounds of what is permitted under § 107 or § 108 concerning copyrighted sound recordings would be actionable under state law with respect to pre-1972 sound recordings. Indeed, it is unlikely that such activities would even elicit a claim.

What should the state law survey address? Concerning state criminal laws, among the issues to be explored are (1) What specific conduct concerning pre-1972 sound recordings is prohibited under state laws? (2) Do any states criminalize conduct performed for reasons other than profit or private financial gain, or imply such motive from the value of works copied or distributed without authorization?[113] (3) What is the significance of the exemption for not-for-for profit and governmental institutions in California's record piracy law? What significance, if any, does it have in other states whose criminal laws are similarly worded but lack a similar exemption?

Concerning civil liability, important questions to be investigated include (1) Are there statutes or cases related to civil protection of pre-1972 sound recordings, and what is the scope of that protection? (2) To what extent have state courts looked to federal copyright law to inform decisions concerning sound recordings? (3) Do "unfair competition," "misappropriation," or similar torts that might be as-

---

[113] *Cf.* 17 U.S.C. § 506(a).

serted extend to conduct that causes financial harm to the right holder, even though it may not be done for, or result in, profit to the user?

Finally, one must bear in mind that while the focus of this report is dissemination by digital streaming, there are other ways in which a library might disseminate pre-1972 sound recordings. No analog transmissions or broadcasts are covered by the sound recording performance right for copyrighted sound recordings, and we assume that right holders of pre-1972 sound recordings do not regard analog performances as within the scope of their rights (or do not regard them as an economic threat), since radio stations make analog transmissions every day, and we are not aware of any claims.[114] Thus, if digital transmissions are not implicated, it appears that only rights in the underlying works would have to be obtained for analog transmissions, and where the underlying works are musical compositions, that can be achieved with blanket licenses from the performing rights societies. (Of course, no license is necessary for musical compositions in the public domain, such as the Mahler, Telemann, and Bach compositions in examples 2, 4, and 5, above.)

5. Technological Protection Issues

The Digital Millennium Copyright Act (DMCA) prohibits the act of circumventing a technological measure that "effectively controls access" to a work protected by copyright.[115] "Technological access controls" are mechanisms such as passwords or encryption that prevent viewing or listening to the work without authorization.

The law also contains two "antitrafficking" provisions. The first is aimed at devices and services that circumvent technological access controls. It prohibits manufacturing, importing, offering to the public, providing, or otherwise trafficking in technologies, products or services that
1. are primarily designed or produced to circumvent a technological measure that effectively controls access to a copyrighted work, or
2. have only limited commercially significant purpose or use other than to circumvent such controls, or
3. are marketed for use in circumventing such controls.[116]

There is a similarly worded prohibition against trafficking in devices or services to circumvent rights controls.[117] "Technological rights controls" are mechanisms that restrict copying the work or playing it in a particular environment without authorization. There is no prohibition on the act of circumventing rights controls. If one circumvents rights controls to infringe, then there is copyright-in-

---

[114] If, however, high-quality, efficient nondigital "on-demand" transmissions to individual users could be technologically achieved, it might raise concerns for right holders under state laws.

[115] § 1201(a)(1)(A).

[116] § 1201(a)(2).

[117] § 1201(b).

fringement liability but no liability for the circumvention; if one circumvents rights controls to exercise a privilege under copyright, there is no liability under copyright or for the circumvention.

There are some exceptions to these "anticircumvention" laws, but for the most part the exceptions are narrow. There is no exception for archiving, nor is there a general "fair use" type exception written into the statute.[118] The law does, however, include an administrative procedure for creating new exemptions. Every three years, the Copyright Office conducts a rule-making proceeding to determine whether users of any particular class(es) of copyrighted works are, or are likely to be, adversely affected in their ability to make noninfringing uses of those works by the prohibition against circumventing technological access controls. If so, the Librarian of Congress, upon the Copyright Office's recommendation, lifts the prohibition on circumventing access controls for those classes of works for the ensuing three-year period.

The DMCA applies to copyrighted works, which in the case of pre-1972 sound recordings would include the underlying musical or other works still in copyright and pre-1972 sound recordings of foreign origin whose copyrights have been restored. The DMCA could potentially affect archiving in a couple of ways. First, the law would prohibit an archives from circumventing technological access controls to obtain access to copyrighted works. If an archives has legally defensible reasons for seeking to circumvent access controls, it could seek an exemption pursuant to the rule-making procedure discussed above. One of the exemptions granted in the most recent rule making addressed such a situation. The Internet Archive submitted evidence that its efforts to transfer computer programs and video games on obsolete media to a computer system for storage and preservation were stymied because the access controls accompanying those works required the original media to be present for the works to function. The exemption allows circumvention of the access controls on such works.[119]

The second potential problem is the DMCA's ban on the circulation of circumvention devices. Even where a library or an archives has valid access to a work, that work may be protected by a copy control. Circumventing the copy control will not violate the DMCA (its permissibility would be judged separately under the Copyright Act), but a library or an archives may not have the means readily available to make that copy because of the antitrafficking provision.

Technological protections are a potential hindrance to certain library preservation and replacement activities and may require a legislative solution rather than resort to the limited relief that the

---

[118] There is an exception that permits a nonprofit library, archive, or educational institution to circumvent a technological access control to make a good faith determination whether to acquire a copy of the protected work. However, the institution may not retain that copy longer than necessary to make that determination, nor use it for any other purpose. § 1201(d).

[119] Copyright Office: Exemption to Prohibition on Circumvention of Copyright Protection Systems for Access Control Technologies, Final Rule, 68 Fed. Reg. 62,011 at 62,014 (October 31, 2003).

Copyright Office can provide through the rule-making mechanism. However, technological measures do not appear to be an obstacle to preservation of pre-1972 sound recordings, since such measures have been employed on phonorecords only recently with the advent of digital technology, and even now are not widely used.[120]

The anticircumvention provisions of the DMCA have no relevance to a pre-1972 U.S. sound recording of a public domain work, as no work protected by federal copyright law is involved.

6. Conclusion

Preservation efforts with respect to pre-1972 sound recordings are hampered by legal restrictions. For example, a work is considered to be in an "obsolete" format, eligible for preservation copying, only if the device necessary to play it is no longer "commercially available." Under this formulation, even LP and 78-rpm records are not eligible for copying as "obsolete," since turntables can still be purchased, even though they are no longer commonly used.

Preservation efforts are also hindered by significant ambiguities in the law. State laws govern copying and dissemination of pre-1972 sound recordings. A detailed survey, to be conducted by the National Recording Preservation Board, will likely clarify the scope of state criminal laws, but given the amorphous nature of common law and the variations among states, considerable uncertainty about what is allowable under the civil law of the various states is likely to remain, even after the survey is completed.

How should a library or an archives proceed with its preservation mission in the face of such obstacles? One way is to identify and design projects where the risk of infringing on third-party rights (and the risk of suit) is relatively low. For example, a project might make digital copies for long-term preservation but not for current dissemination; focus on older sound recordings, on those with no identifiable right holder, or on those with underlying works in the public domain; establish an "opt-out" mechanism for right holders; stream only small portions of sound recordings; stream only to specific locations, such as other libraries or archives; and/or stream only to specific users, such as preauthorized music scholars. Some combination of such features could reduce the risk of commercial harm to the right holder and increase the likelihood that the activity would be deemed privileged if a claim were to be asserted. This approach can be time-intensive, however, as it requires careful development of projects and regular monitoring to ensure that project guidelines are

---

[120] It is possible that a pre-1972 sound recording of a public domain work might be digitally remastered and rereleased with technological protection. If there is sufficient new authorship to entitle the new sound recording to protection as a derivative work, the library could circumvent technological access controls only pursuant to a statutory exception in § 1201, but could circumvent rights controls to exercise any copyright privilege, provided it could find a means to circumvent. If there is not sufficient new authorship, then there is no copyright-protected work and no legal bar to circumventing access controls or rights controls.

adhered to and, in many cases, legal and factual research to determine the copyright status of subject works.[121]

A library must carefully consider the degree of risk that it wishes to undertake (e.g., whether it wants to stretch the limits of the law). The Library of Congress, for example, is likely to come under closer scrutiny than other institutions do, both by libraries and archives searching for guidance in their own preservation and dissemination programs and by right holders whose works are used without express authorization. The Library of Congress has traditionally been very cognizant of copyright rights in serving its patrons (it is, after all, home to the Copyright Office) and presumably will continue to be so.

A risk-management approach may provide a useful means of preserving or disseminating some works and a possible basis for moving forward with limited pilot programs to help determine the administrative, technical, and legal feasibility of digital preservation initiatives. However, a comprehensive program to digitize and stream pre-1972 sound recordings would likely require some combination of obtaining licenses,[122] entering into other cooperative agreements with right holders,[123] and legislative change.

Legislative change is critical to enable responsible and efficient digital preservation and dissemination activities with respect to pre-1972 sound recordings, as even our limited review of state laws demonstrates. The necessity for legislative change to enable preservation activities is not limited to pre-1972 sound recordings: it cuts across a wide range of other copyright-protected works. The copyright law has historically granted special privileges to libraries and archives to enable preservation of our cultural and intellectual heritage, and there is every reason to believe that it will continue to adapt to preserve these privileges in the digital world, balancing the needs of libraries and archives with the legitimate interests of right holders. A new study group has been formed to consider the exceptions for libraries and archives in the copyright law and to make recommendations by mid-2006 for possible changes to reflect new technologies.[124] As the effort to reformulate library privileges for the digital age moves forward, the focus of attention is likely to be the special

[121] For example, identifying the copyright status of works, their country of origin, and when they were published—not to mention their commercial availability—are time-consuming tasks.

[122] Entering into licenses to permit streaming would provide certainty with respect to certain works, but could be expensive. It may also require paying for uses that, as a matter of public policy, a library should be entitled to make. Given the current uncertainty in the industry concerning issues related to on-demand streaming of copyrighted works, it is impossible to assess the potential cost of such licenses.

[123] Collaborative preservation agreements with sound recording copyright owners are another possibility. There is some precedent for this in the motion picture industry, and it would have the possible advantage of achieving library access to, and preservation of, copies of sound recordings that are currently under the exclusive control of record companies.

[124] "Section 108 Study Group Convenes to Discuss Exceptions to Copyright Law for Libraries and Archives," (May 13, 2005), at http://www.loc.gov/today/pr/2005/05-121.html.

privileges granted to libraries in § 108 of the copyright law. Libraries would, for example, benefit from more flexible standards for digital copying that would allow them to keep pace with evolving best practices for digital preservation. It is important to bear in mind, however, that changes to § 108 will not resolve state law issues. Those issues will have to be addressed by altering, in some measure, the "carve out" from federal preemption that § 301(c) of the Copyright Act accords to state laws related to pre-1972 sound recordings.

Appendix

Results of Preliminary Research Concerning State Law

A. California

1. *Criminal Law.* California's criminal record piracy statute was enacted in 1968. The law provides, in relevant part, that a person is guilty of the offense if he:

> Knowingly and willfully transfers or causes to be transferred any sounds that have been recorded on a phonograph record, disc, wire, tape, film or other article on which sounds are recorded, with intent to sell or cause to be sold, or to use or cause to be used for commercial advantage or private financial gain through public performance, the article on which the sounds are so transferred, without the consent of the owner.[1]

There is an exemption for not-for-profit educational institutions or federal or state governmental entities that meet certain conditions. The entity

- must have "as a primary purpose the advancement of the public's knowledge and the dissemination of information regarding America's musical cultural heritage," and that purpose must be "clearly set forth in the institution's or entity's charter, bylaws," or similar document;[2] and

- may avail itself of the exemption if, prior to the transfer, it makes "a good faith effort to identify and locate the owner or owners of the sound recordings to be transferred," and "the owner or owners could not be and have not been located."[3]

The exemption goes on to state:

> Nothing in this section shall be construed to relieve an institution or entity of its contractual or other obligation to compensate the owners of sound recordings to be transferred. In order to continue the exemption permitted by this subdivision, the

---

[1] Cal. Penal Code § 653h (2004). See also *Goldstein v. California*, 412 U.S. 546 (1973) (concluding that state protection of pre-1972 sound recordings was not preempted by federal copyright law).

[2] *Id.* § 653h(h).

[3] *Id.*

institution or entity shall make continuing efforts to locate such owners and shall make an annual public notice of the fact of the transfers in newspapers of general circulation serving the jurisdictions where the owners were incorporated or doing business at the time of initial affixations. The institution or entity shall keep on file a record of the efforts made to locate such owners for inspection by appropriate governmental agencies.[4]

2. *Civil Law.* California's civil protection of pre-1972 sound record-ings, § 980(a)(2), provides:

The author of an original work of authorship consisting of a sound recording initially fixed prior to February 15, 1972, has an exclusive ownership therein until February 15, 2047, as against all persons except one who independently makes or duplicates another sound recording that does not directly or indirectly recapture the actual sounds fixed in such prior sound recording, but consists entirely of an independent fixation of other sounds, even though such sounds imitate or simulate the sounds contained in the prior sound recording.[5]

The civil statute does not include an exemption similar to the criminal statute for not-for-profit, educational, or governmental insti-tutions, or for any other uses.

The few cases decided under § 980(a)(2) have viewed the section as conferring an intangible property interest in the sound recordings that can be protected in a misappropriation, conversion or unfair competition claim.[6] They have dealt predominantly with for-profit entities that have copied sound recordings without authorization and therefore do not provide guidance as to how not-for-profit entities or uses of such recordings will be treated. They have, however, distinguished the property interest protected by state law from copyright law by stating that these actions lie outside copyright (and, arguably, outside the realm of copyright defenses).[7]

The only case we found addressing the use of pre-1972 sound recordings for educational purposes was *Bridge Publications, Inc. v. Vien*.[8] The defendant violated § 980(a)(2) by copying tape-recorded lectures by L. Ron Hubbard without authorization. Although the

---

[4] *Id.*

[5] Cal. Civ. Code § 980(a)(2)(2004).

[6] For example, *Lone Ranger Television, Inc. v. Program Radio Corp.*, 740 F.2d 718, 725 (9th Cir. 1984) (addressing conversion claim of intangible property rights in sound recordings); *A & M Records, Inc. v. Heilman*, 75 Cal. App. 3d 554, 570 (Cal. Ct. App. 1977) ("These recorded performances are A & M Records' intangible personal property. . . . [The] misappropriation and sale of the intangible property of another without authority from the owner is conversion.").

[7] See *Lone Ranger*, 740 F.2d at 726 ("Lone Ranger TV's protection against conversion of an intangible property right in the performances embodied in its tapes is unaffected by notions of copyright"); *A & M Records*, 75 Cal. App. 3d at 564 ("A & M Records' action against Heilman for duplicating without consent *performances* embodied in A & M Records' recordings is independent of any action that the owners of the underlying compositions might bring against Heilman for copyright infringement.").

[8] 827 F. Supp. 629 (S.D. Cal. 1993).

copying of the pre-1972 sound recordings was related to education (defendant's course on "Dynamism"), the court found that the use was commercial in nature because the course was "offered for sale."[9]

However, because case law related to § 980(a)(2) and earlier common law protection of sound recordings have focused primarily on the for-profit motives of defendants in finding liability under theories of unfair competition and misappropriation, a court could reach a different conclusion if the use were purely educational and not-for-profit.

B. Illinois

1. *Criminal Law.* The Illinois criminal code provides that "[a] person commits unlawful use of recorded sounds or images when he":

> Intentionally, knowingly or recklessly transfers or causes to be transferred without the consent of the owner, any sounds or images recorded on any sound or audio visual recording with the purpose of selling or causing to be sold, or using or causing to be used for profit the article to which such sounds or recordings of sound are transferred.[10]

The law also prohibits

- intentionally selling or advertising the unauthorized copies for sale, or using them or causing them to be used for profit; and

- intentionally offering or making available for a "fee, rental, or any other form of compensation, directly or indirectly" any equipment for the purpose of reproducing any sound or audiovisual recording without the owner's consent.[11]

No specific exception for not-for-profit use is included in the statute. No cases have been decided under this section of the code.[12]

2. *Civil Law.* In *Capitol Records, Inc. v. Spies*,[13] the court held that pirating sound recordings and selling the pirated versions for profit is considered unfair competition and wrongful appropriation. The defendant purchased records in retail stores, then made and sold 1,500 unauthorized copies. The court found this to be unfair competition. It did not explicitly make commercial gain an element of an unfair competition claim, but the defendant in that case had profited from his piracy.

---

9 *Id.* at 632.

10 § 720 Ill. Comp. Stat. Ann. 5/16–7 (1) (2004).

11 § 720 Ill. Comp. Stat. Ann. 5/16–7 (2), (3) (2004).

12 Only a couple of reported cases cite this section, and they provide little guidance. See *Gardner v. Senior Living Sys.*, 731 N.E. 2d 350 (Ill. App. Ct. 2000) (stating in dicta that former employee's failure to remove company software from a computer that she had absconded with would be a violation of the law prohibiting unlawful use of recorded sounds or images); *People v. Zakarian*, 460 N.E. 2d 422 (Ill. App. Ct. 1984) (addressing whether a similarly worded predecessor statute encompassed unlawful use of unidentified sounds).

13 264 N.E.2d 874 (Ill. App. Ct. 1970).

As explained by a subsequent Illinois court decision, "underlying the court's reasoning [in *Spies*] is the premise that the plaintiff's pecuniary reward for producing its intangible product would be severely reduced if other competitors could avoid production costs by merely waiting until a record became popular and then recording the work for resale."[14]

There were no cases in which the defendant had used the contested sound recording for a nonprofit purpose.

Other Illinois unfair competition cases outside the sound recording context similarly do not explicitly state that commercial exploitation by the defendant is required to make a valid claim. Nevertheless, they all arise in a commercial context, and invariably the defendant had gained commercially from appropriating the plaintiff's property right.[15]

C. Michigan

1. *Criminal Law.* Michigan's record piracy statute prohibits a person from transferring (or causing to be transferred), without the consent of the owner, a sound recording, "with the intent to sell or cause to be sold for profit or used to promote the sale of a product, the article on which the sound is so transferred."[16] It also prohibits knowingly advertising or selling the unauthorized copies.[17]

The law contains the following exclusion for persons who transfer sound:

    a. intended for or in connection with radio or television broadcast transmission or related uses;

    b. for archival, library, or educational purposes; or

    c. solely for the personal use of the person transferring or causing the transfer and without any compensation being derived by the person from the transfer.[18]

No cases have been decided under or interpret this portion of Michigan's code.

2. *Civil Law.* We found only one case that directly addressed unauthorized reproduction and distribution of pre-1972 sound recordings

---

14 *Bd. of Trade of City of Chi. v. Dow Jones & Co.*, 456 N.E. 2d 84, 88 (Ill. 1983).

15 See, e.g., *Delta Medical Systems v. Mid-America Medical Systems, Inc.*, 772 N.E. 2d 768 (Ill. App. Ct. 2002) (reversing lower court decision granting preliminary injunction on claim that defendant misappropriated plaintiff's trade secrets in order to set up and operate a competing business); *Everen Securities, Inc. v. A.G. Edwards and Sons, Inc.*, 719 N.E. 2d 312 (Ill. App. Ct. 1999) (affirming arbitration panel's award to plaintiff where defendants, former employees of plaintiff, solicited plaintiff's customers and photocopied plaintiff's customer records for the purpose of creating a database for their new employer).

16 Mich. Comp. Laws Ann. § 752.782 (West 2004).

17 *Id*. § 752.783.

18 *Id*. § 752.785.

in Michigan. In *A & M Records, Inc. v. M.V. C. Distributing Corp.*,[19] the U.S. Court of Appeals for the Sixth Circuit upheld the district court's conclusion that unauthorized duplication and distribution of sound recordings constituted unfair competition under the common law of Michigan. The case does not discuss the cause of action in detail.

Michigan unfair competition cases outside the sound recording context have consistently involved commercial exploitation of plaintiff's property right by the defendant, although never is this specifically made a requirement of the unfair competition claim.[20] Our review did not reveal cases in which defendant was not seeking to profit commercially from the appropriation of the plaintiff's property right.

D. New York

1. *Criminal Law.* New York Penal Law provides criminal liability for a person who

1. knowingly, and without the consent of the owner, transfers or causes to be transferred any sound recording, with the intent to rent or sell, or cause to be rented or sold for profit, or used to promote the sale of any product, such article to which such recording was transferred, or

2. transports within this state, for commercial advantage or private financial gain, a recording, knowing that the sounds have been reproduced or transferred without the consent of the owner.[21]

However, there are exceptions in the law for "any broadcaster who . . . for the purpose of archival preservation, transfers any such recorded sounds or images" and for "any person who transfers such sounds or images for personal use, and without profit for such transfer."[22] The statute does not define the terms "broadcaster" or "archival preservation." There is no case law on this subsection that helps clarify those terms.

2. *Civil Law.* New York has a substantial body of case law applying common law principles of unfair competition to those who make and distribute unauthorized copies of sound recordings. One court described the elements of an unfair competition claim as follows: (1) plaintiff must establish a property right of commercial value;

---

[19] 574 F.2d 312 (1978). But see *Artie Field Prods. v. Channel 7*, 1994 U.S. Dist. Lexis 16828 (D. Mich. June 10, 1994) (stating in dicta that A & M Records' claim would have been preempted had it arisen after § 301 became effective).

[20] See, e.g., *Thrifty Acres, Inc. v. Al-Naimi*, 326 N.W.2d 400 (Mich. Ct. App. 1982) (court affirmed lower court ruling in favor of plaintiff who brought unfair competition claim against defendant who had begun operating a grocery store under a trade name established by plaintiff grocery store operator).

[21] N.Y. CLS Penal § 275.05 (2004).

[22] *Id.* § 275.45.

and (2) plaintiff must prove that defendant appropriated that property right for *commercial gain*.[23]

None of the other New York unfair competition cases involving pre-1972 sound recordings states explicitly that commercial gain by defendant is a required element. They simply state that production and distribution of unauthorized copies constitute unfair competition.[24] Notably, one court has stated that the scope of protection under unfair competition was broad enough to encompass "any form of unfair invasion or infringement and . . . any form of commercial immorality."[25] This suggests that an invasion of another's property right that causes commercial harm (even though not for commercial gain) could give rise to an unfair competition claim.[26] Other courts have been similarly broad in crafting the unfair competition standard: "[Where] the apparent purpose is to reap where one has not sown, or to gather where one has not planted, or to build upon, or [to] profit from, the name, reputation, good will or work of another such actions will be enjoined as unfair competition."[27] However, all the unfair competition cases involving record piracy involved defendants who were seeking to use the pirated sound recording for commercial gain.[28] While unfair competition claims commonly involve direct competition between plaintiff and defendant, direct competition is not essential to a claim.[29]

In *Arista Records, Inc. v. MP3Board, Inc.*,[30] the court denied MP3Board's motion for summary judgment on plaintiff record companies' suit. MP3Board operated an Internet site that provided users with pirated copies of the record companies' musical recordings. The

---

[23] *Rostropovich v. Koch Int'l. Corp.*, 34 U.S.P.Q.2d (BNA) 1609 (S.D.N.Y. 1995).

[24] See, e.g., *Greater Recording Co., Inc. v. Stambler*, 144 U.S.P.Q. 547 (N.Y. Sup. Ct. 1965) (denying motion to dismiss where defendant allegedly produced and distributed records made directly from plaintiffs' recordings); *Capitol Records, Inc. v. Greatest Records, Inc.*, 43 Misc. 2d 878 (N.Y. Sup. Ct. 1964) (enjoining defendant from manufacturing and distributing record album containing identical reproductions of certain records sold by plaintiff).

[25] *Metro. Opera Ass'n. v. Wagner-Nichols Recorder Corp.*, 101 N.Y.S.2d 483, 492 (N.Y. Sup. Ct. 1950), *order affirmed*, 279 A.D. 632, 107 N.Y.S.2d 795 (1st Dep't 1951).

[26] See *Metro. Opera*, 101 N.Y.S.2d at 492 ("[U]nfair competition . . . rest[s] . . . on the . . . broader principle that property rights of commercial value are to be and will be protected. . .").

[27] *Apple Corps, Ltd. v. Adirondack Group*, 124 Misc. 2d 351, 354 (N.Y. Sup. Ct., 1983) (quoting *Harvey Mach. Co. v Harvey Aluminum Corp.*, 9 Misc. 2d 1078, 1080 (N.Y. Sup. Ct. 1957).

[28] See, e.g., *Roy Export Co. v. Columbia Broadcasting System, Inc.*, 672 F.2d 1095, 1105 (2d Cir. 1982) ("[Defendant] unquestionably appropriated the 'skill, expenditures and labor' of the plaintiffs to its own commercial advantage. We are confident that the New York courts would call this conduct unfair competition"); *Capitol Records*, 43 Misc. 2d 878, 881 (N.Y. Sup. Ct. 1964) (granting plaintiff's motion for temporary injunction where defendant had made phonograph records by copying tape recordings made by plaintiff and sold the records to the public); *Radio Corp. of America v. Premier Albums, Inc.*, 19 A.D.2d 62, 64 (N.Y. App. Div., 1963) (granting plaintiff's motion for an injunction because defendant's continued "[u]nrestrained commercial exploitation, competitively, would result in irreparable harm to [plaintiff] and render the right of little value.").

[29] *Id.* at 491–92 ("[T]he existence of actual competition between the parties is no longer a prerequisite [to an unfair competition claim.]").

[30] 2002 U.S. Dist. Lexis 16165 (S.D.N.Y. August. 28, 2002).

record companies brought suit for copyright infringement with respect to the post-1972 sound recordings and for common law unfair competition with respect to the pre-1972 recordings. Concerning the state law claims, the court stated:

> In New York, an unfair competition claim may be grounded in the appropriation of the exclusive property of the plaintiff by the defendant. Pursuant to New York common law, "an unfair competition claim involving misappropriation usually concerns the taking and use of the plaintiff's property to compete against the plaintiff's own use of the same property." Due to the legal overlap between the New York tort of unfair competition based upon misappropriation and federal copyright infringement, summary judgment in favor of MP3Board is denied for the reasons stated above denying summary judgment on the copyright infringement claims.[31]

Despite the discussion of "unfair competition" in earlier claims under New York common law involving pre-1972 sound recordings, the New York Court of Appeals recently ruled that "common law copyright" applies to those sound recordings, and distinguished that tort from unfair competition. *Capitol Records, Inc. v. Naxos of America, Inc.*[32] involved recordings of performances of classical music that were made in England in the 1930s by Yehudi Menuhin, Pablo Casals, and Edwin Fischer. Capitol succeeded to the rights in those recordings in the United States. When Naxos, without a license from Capitol, remastered and sold copies of the recordings in the United States, Capitol sued in federal district court. The district court found in favor of Naxos, on grounds, among other things, that the works were in the public domain in New York since they were in the public domain in England.[33] On appeal, the Second Circuit determined that the case involved state law issues of first impression and certified several questions of law to the New York Court of Appeals, the highest court in New York.[34] The New York Court of Appeals' recent decision held that there was no reason for New York to adopt another country's term of protection, and that New York law protected the

---

[31] *Id.* at *36–*37 (citations omitted).

[32] 4 N.Y.3d 540 (2005).

[33] 274 F. Supp.2d 472 (S.D.N.Y. 2003).

[34] 372 F.3d 471 (2d Cir. 2004). The Second Circuit certified the following questions to the New York Court of Appeals:

"In view of the District Court's assessment of the undisputed facts, but without regard to the issue of abandonment, is Naxos entitled to defeat Capitol's claim for infringement of common law copyrights in the original recordings?" This overall question subsumes the following sub-questions: (1) "Does the expiration of the term of a copyright in the country of origin terminate a common law copyright in New York?" (2) "Does a cause of action for common law copyright infringement include some or all of the elements of unfair competition?" (3) "Is a claim of common law copyright infringement defeated by a defendant's showing that the plaintiff's work has slight if any current market and that the defendant's work, although using components of the plaintiff's work, is fairly to be regarded as a 'new product'?" Id. at 484–85.

recordings, regardless of whether they were in the public domain in England.[35]

In its decision, the court also clarified the nature of common law copyright in New York, stating that a claim "consists of two elements: (1) the existence of a valid copyright; and (2) unauthorized reproduction of the work protected by copyright." The court made it clear that bad faith is not an element of a common law infringement claim in New York,[36] and that:

> Copyright infringement is distinguishable from unfair competition, which in addition to unauthorized copying and distribution requires competition in the marketplace or similar actions designed for commercial benefit.[37]

The final question certified by the Second Circuit related to the significance of a showing that Capitol's recordings have "slight if any current market," and that Naxos's work, because of the remastering, "is fairly to be regarded as a new product." The New York court held that the size of the market or the popularity of a product does not affect the ability to enforce a state law copyright claim. It observed, with reference to federal copyright law, that Naxos's recordings were not independent creations and that under the fair use doctrine, reproduction of an entire work is generally infringing.[38] It ruled that even if Naxos created a "new product" through remastering, that product could still infringe Capitol's copyright "to the extent that it utilizes the original elements of the protected performances."[39]

E. Virginia

1. *Criminal Law.* Virginia law provides that it is unlawful to:

> Knowingly transfer or cause to be transferred, directly or indirectly by any means . . . any sounds recorded on a phonograph record, disc, wire, tape, film, videocassette, or other article now known or later developed on which sounds are recorded, with the intent to sell, rent or cause to be sold or rented, or to be used for profit through public performance, such article on which sounds are so transferred, without consent of the owner.[40]

It is also an offense, for commercial advantage or private financial gain, to:

> Manufacture, distribute, transport or wholesale, or cause to be manufactured, distributed, transported or sold as wholesale, or

---

[35] 4 N.Y.3d at 561–63.

[36] *Id.* at 563.

[37] *Id.* (citations omitted).

[38] *Id.* at 564.

[39] *Id.* at 564–65.

[40] Va. Code Ann. § 59.1–41.2(1) (Michie 2004).

possess for such purposes any article with the knowledge that the sounds are so transferred, without consent of the owner.[41]

There is an exception for persons engaged in radio and television broadcasting to copy sound recordings for use in connection with their broadcast or for related uses, "or for archival purposes."[42] There is no specific exception for not-for-profit use. There is one citing reference to this section.[43]

2. *Civil Law.* We were unable to find any unfair competition cases in Virginia that deal with unauthorized reproduction and distribution of sound recordings.

Outside the context of sound recordings, no Virginia case explicitly makes commercial exploitation an element of an unfair competition claim. However, all Virginia's unfair competition cases involve some form of commercial exploitation by the defendant.[44]

---

[41] *Id.* § 59.1-41.2(2).

[42] *Id.* § 59.1-41.2.

[43] *Milteer v. Commonwealth*, 267 Va. 732, 595 S.E.2d 275 (2004) (court affirmed conviction of defendant for knowingly possessing pirated videocassettes for the purpose of selling them).

[44] See, e.g., *Cimmarron's Old South Corp. v. Traveller's Alley Café, Inc.*, 18 Va. Cir. 436 (Va. Cir. Ct. 1990) (preliminary injunction granted where plaintiff brought claim for unfair competition in the use of trade names against restaurant located on same street as his restaurant); *Craigie, Inc. v. Legg Mason Wood Walker, Inc.*, 20 Va. Cir. 342 (Va. Cir. Ct. 1990) (arbitration panel's award to plaintiff confirmed where plaintiff's unfair competition claim was based on allegation that defendant illegally induced plaintiff's employees to leave plaintiff's firm and work for defendant's firm).